AF479120

Columbia Themes in Philosophy, Social Criticism, and the Arts

Sacred Exchanges

Columbia Themes in Philosophy, Social Criticism, and the Arts

COLUMBIA THEMES IN PHILOSOPHY, SOCIAL CRITICISM, AND THE ARTS PRESENTS monographs, essay collections, and short books on philosophy and aesthetic theory. It aims to publish books that show the ability of the arts to stimulate critical reflection on modern and contemporary social, political, and cultural life. Art is not now, if it ever was, a realm of human activity independent of the complex realities of social organization and change, political authority and antagonism, cultural domination and resistance. The possibilities of critical thought embedded in the arts are most fruitfully expressed when addressed to readers across the various fields of social and humanistic inquiry. The idea of philosophy in the series title ought to be understood, therefore, to embrace forms of discussion that begin where mere academic expertise exhausts itself, where the rules of social, political, and cultural practice are both affirmed and challenged, and where new thinking takes place. The series does not privilege any particular art, nor does it ask for the arts to be mutually isolated. The series encourages writing from the many fields of thoughtful and critical inquiry. For a list of titles in the series, see page 171.

Sacred Exchanges

Images in Global Context

ROBYN FERRELL

Columbia University Press ✦ NEW YORK

Columbia University Press
Publishers Since 1893
New York,   Chichester, West Sussex

Library of Congress Cataloging-in-Publication Data

Ferrell, Robyn, 1960–
 Sacred exchanges : images in global context / Robyn Ferrell.
    p. cm. — (Columbia themes in philosophy, social criticism, and the arts)
 Includes bibliographical references and index.
 ISBN 978-0-231-14880-1 (cloth : alk. paper)
 1. Art—Political aspects.   2. Art—Economic aspects.   3. Art and society.
 4. Painting, Aboriginal Australian.   I. Title.

N72.P6F47 2012
700.1—dc23

2011025622

CONTENTS

Acknowledgments   vii
List of Photographs   xi

Writing on Art   1

Art   7
Utopia   7
Dreaming   8
Abstraction   17
Striking Color   19
The Real Power of Color   25
How Painting Began   27

Culture   45
Global Art, Local Knowledge   45
The Idea of the Museum   52
In Translation   58
A White Thing   62
Image Logic   64
Photojournalism   68

Gender   75

Stolen Culture   76

Little Children Are Sacred   79

Mum's the Word   84

Crisis in Representation   91

Race and Gender   96

Law   99

Common Law   106

Feeling for Justice   112

Apartheid   116

Discovery   123

Radical Difference   131

Emily Inc.   144

References   153

Index   161

ACKNOWLEDGMENTS

I would like to thank many people for their help, formal and informal, with the writing of this book: Vivien Anderson, Michelle Andringa, Frances Andrijich, Jennifer Biddle, Larry Boyd, Barbara Caine, Tina Chanter, Ros Diprose, Kathleen Fallon, John Frow, Moira Gatens, Anna Gibbs, Christine Godden, Julie Gough, Ricardo Idagi, Stacy Keltner, Mary Knights, Libby Lester, Des Manderson, Mike McMahon, Djon Mundine, Christine Nicholls, Kelly Oliver, Julie Oster, Hetti Perkins, Elspeth Probyn, Cassandra Pybus, Helen Read, Judith Ryan, Jon von Sturmer, and Ewa Ziarek.

Thanks to family, Jo and Richard, Rose and Pete, Pat and Rob, John and Margaret, and Peninsula friends Anne and Bronwyn for their active support.

I am especially grateful to Lynnette, Molly, Myra, Rosie, and Lily for their generous engagement, across "language" and country, at the workshop at the College of Fine Arts, University of New South Wales in 2007. Thanks also to Waringarri, Mangkaja, Warmun, Warnayaka, Ikuntji, and Warlayirti Art Centres for their time, and for permission to reproduce photographs of the artists. Maria Trochatos and Pamela Turton-Turner gave valuable help as research assistants.

Research for this book was largely funded by the Australian Research Council, and work in progress received support from Vanderbilt University, Tennessee; the Gender Institute at the London School of Economics and Politics, London; University of Western Sydney; University of New South Wales; Australian National University; and Macquarie University.

Earlier versions of some material appeared in *Cultural Studies Review, Studies in Practical Philosophy, Law Text Culture* and Oliver and Keltner (2009).

Finally, I want to acknowledge the Bunurong people of the Mornington Peninsula, whose traditional country I lived on while writing this book.

Art and Artists

Aboriginal acrylic painting is easily viewed on the web. The weblinks listed below include work of artists and art centers mentioned in this book.

Art Centers

Desart, Alice Springs, Central Desert http://www.desart.com.au
Ikuntji, Haasts Bluff, Central Desert http://www.ikuntji.com.au
Jirrawun, Wyndham, Kimberley http://www.jirrawunarts.com
Mangkaja, Fitzroy Crossing, Kimberley http://www.mangkaja.com
Waringarri, Kununurra, Kimberley http://www.waringarriarts.com.au
Warlayirti, Balgo, Western Desert http://www.balgoart.org.au
Warmun, Turkey Creek, Kimberley, http://www.warmunart.com
Warnayaka, Lajamanu, Central Desert http://warnayaka.com

Public Collections

National Gallery of Australia, Canberra http://nga.gov.au
National Gallery of Victoria, Melbourne http://www.ngv.vic.gov.au/

Art Gallery of New South Wales, Sydney http://www.artgallery
  .nsw.gov.au
Museum of Contemporary Art http://www.mca.com.au
Art Gallery of West Australia http://www.artgallery.wa.gov.au/
Art Gallery of South Australia
http://www.artgallery.sa.gov.au/agsa/home/Collection/
Queensland Art Gallery
http://qag.qld.gov.au/collection/indigenous_australian_ art
Musée du quai Branly, Paris http://www.quaibranly.fr/en
AAMU, Museum of Contemporary Aboriginal Art, Utrecht
  http://www.aamu.nl

Artists

Agnes Armstrong http://www.waringarriarts.com.au
Paddy Bedford http://www.jirrawunarts.com; http://cs.nga.gov.au
http://www.moragalleries.com.au/pbedford/
Julie Dowling http://cs.nga.gov.au
http://www.artplace.com.au/CVs/julie_dowling.html
Peggy Griffiths http://www.waringarriarts.com.au
Lily Nungarrayi Hargraves http://warnayaka.com
http://www.stephanieburns.com.au/LilyHargreavesNungarrayi.html
Ricardo Idagi http://cs.nga.gov.au
http://www.vivienandersongallery.com/artists/ricardo_idagi
  /ricardo_idagi.html
Emily Kame Kngwarreye http://cs.nga.gov.au
http:www.nmagov.au/exhibitions/utopia_the_genius_of_emily
  _kame_kngwarreye/
Tracey Moffatt http://cs.nga.gov.au
http://www.roslynoxley9.com.au/artists/26/Tracey_Moffatt/
Eubena Nampitjin http://www.balgoart.org.au http://cs.nga.gov.au
Makinty Napanangka http://cs.nga.gov.au http://www.japingka
  .com.au

Dorothy Napangardi http://cs.nga.gov.au http://www
    .aboriginalartcoop.com.au/
Judy Mengil http://cs.nga.gov.au http://www.waringarriarts.com.au
Phyllis Ningamara http://www.waringarriarts.com.au
Kathleen Petyarre http://cs.nga.gov.au
http://www.gallerieaustralis.com/aspx/kathleen_petyarre.aspx
Rosie Napurrurla Tasman http://warnayaka.com
Clifford Possum Ttapaltjarri http://cs.nga.gov.au
http://www.artgallery.nsw.gov.au/media/archives_2004/clifford
    _possum
Judy Watson http://cs.nga.gov.au
http://qag.qag.qld.gov.au/collection/indigenous_australian_art
    /judy_watson
Yuendumu Doors http://www.aboriginalartonline.com/regions
    /yuendumu-doors.php

Mackerel sky over Tanami Desert   xiv

Mackerel sky over Tanami Desert   xiv

Mountain devil lizard at Kata Tjuta in the Northern Territory   10

Desert country spinifex   14

Saltpans near Lake Mackay, north West Australia   24

Batik shirt   29

Camp dogs   34

Tourist merchandise using "Aboriginal" designs   36

Paintings for sale in an outback art center   48

Airfield at Turkey Creek   51

Tourists on a guided tour in the Kimberley region   57

Dotting up a wheelchair at a tourist park   61

Uluru at sunset   63

Watching the news   67

Warlpiri artists—from left, Rosie Napurrurla Tasman, Myra
    Nungarrayi Herbert, Lily Nungarrayi Hargraves, and Molly
    Napurrurla Tasman—pose for publicity shots before a dancing
    ceremony at the College of Fine Arts, Sydney   74

Peggy Griffiths, Waringarri Arts   78

A tourist poses on the Michael Nelson Jagamara *Possum & Wallaby Dreaming* mural in front of the Australian Parliament House, Canberra   83
The workshop at the College of Fine Arts, Sydney   95
Ricardo Idagi poses with half-finished turtle shell mask   110
Remote community: housing   120
Uluru viewing place   122
Twilight on country   130
"Gija country": flying over the Bungle Bungles in the Kimberley region   135
Crossing the north coast of West Australia   140
Desert grasses   143
Waringarri artist Agnes Armstrong   150
Waringarri artist Judy Mengil   151
Waringarri artist Phyllis Ningamara (bottom)   151

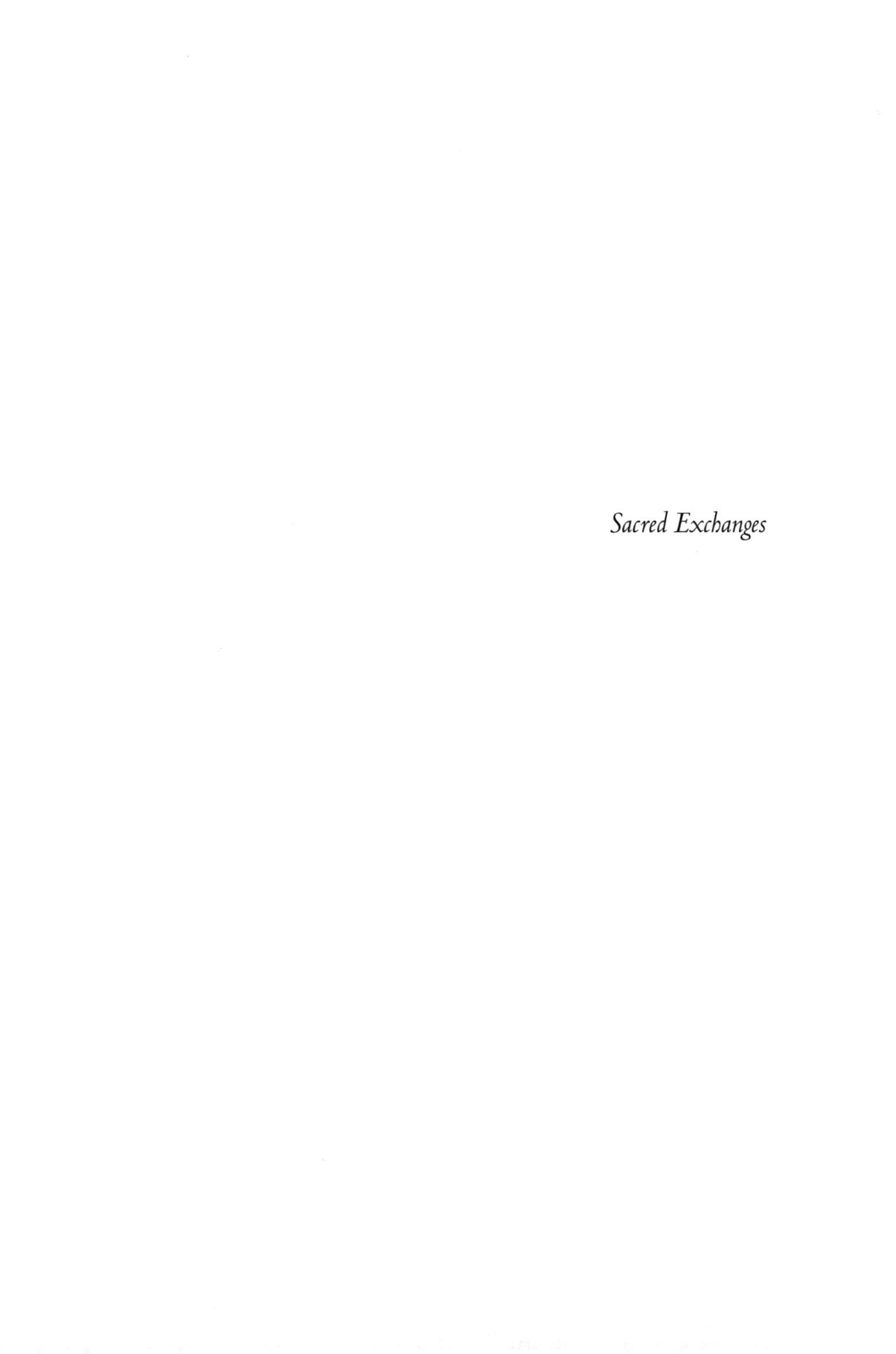

Sacred Exchanges

Writing on Art

No writing on art is ever solely "about" the work it purports to translate, but rather makes of the work an element in its own material. Theory has its own aesthetic, and produces its own crisis. It creates another intelligibility, out of a specific collision of philosophical and artistic materials.

Writing about art does not mean that theory is simply imposed on art, or that artistic ellipsis is merely subjected to critical scrutiny. When theoretical representation attempts to master artistic representation this way, it is most blindly in the grip of its own transferences, and its object typically eludes it.

An example of this is given in this book: the apocalyptic theory of the End of Art that torments philosophical aesthetics. It has been my pleasure to analyze this through the deflating example of Aboriginal acrylic painting and its seeming abstraction.

The figure for theoretical writing *is* abstraction, rather than mastery. Part of my point in writing about artistic abstraction is to continue writing about how we can understand theoretical writing itself as an abstract genre. (I developed this discussion at some length in *Genres of Philosophy*). As John Rachjman observes: "To transform the picture of what it is to think abstractly is to transform the picture of the relations abstract thought may have with the arts" (1995:16).

If the figure of theoretical writing is abstraction, the figure of critical writing is responsibility, not mere judgment. One purpose in writing critically about art, especially Indigenous art now, is the possibility of engaging the political, in its moment of emerging as a legible demand.

The example given here is the case study of contemporary Aboriginal art that, in being also law, has produced its political demand as *painting*. The aesthetic acclaim for this painting has forced recognition of "Real World" rights such as native title to land. The genre of critical writing can uniquely respond to this emerging; it can name it and identify it, it can *represent* it, in political as well as philosophical senses of the word.

This is not thereby a book "about Aboriginal art," or not only about it. In deploying the genres of theoretical and critical writing in a discussion of this painting, in its specific time and place, I have sought to illustrate the habit of representations generally—of words and images—to produce real value.

To adapt a slogan: *aesthetics precedes ethics*. It is the power of images to make a reality that becomes increasingly visible as the contemporary scene becomes more dominated by images (of which artistic images are only a small part). And judgment emerges from the values created, as part of their production. It is toward understanding this ontological conundrum that this writing on art is directed.

Four old Warlpiri women artists and their daughter, granddaughter, and great-granddaughter came down to Sydney from Lajamanu on the edge of the Tanami Desert, for a workshop to paint their *jukurrpa*, their Dreaming.

We set them up in a studio on the top floor of the College of Fine Arts, with a deep balcony and a view to the harbor. They had yards of Belgian linen, liter bottles of acrylic paint, brushes, and bamboo skewers with which to make dots. They were paid by the hour and the resulting paintings they retain as a collection.

This research project invited them to share some women's business through painting some of their traditional designs for our instruction. The results are part of the material that created this book.

Other research and fieldwork were performed over five years in several outback art centers, in international museums and art fairs in Paris, London, New York, Washington, D.C., and Munich, and using the national collections of Aboriginal acrylic painting in various Australian galleries. I spoke with many Indigenous artists, their gallerists, art center advisers, and anthropologists in that time.

This book looks at what art means now, in the global context. It does so through the remarkable case of Aboriginal Desert acrylic painting. Fine art and Indigenous art, applied arts and artifacts—even museums—are dictated by markets that give them value as objects of exchange. But art in Western cultures which fund these markets is also felt to mean more than mere money. The story of the exchange of cultures implied by the success of Desert painting is the subject of this book, but the moral is broader: no less than the significance of the cultural and psychic investments in images per se.

This book explores the politics of producing art within a global economy that shapes international forces and events. It visits different locations in the "Real World," from the Tanami Desert to the Musée du quai Branly, from Bon Marché to the Smithsonian, from Dachau to the Sudan. It traverses the experience of desert communities, where making art is the only alternative to living on welfare, to show how we occupy different positions in the "Real World" of global capital. It explores the history of Aboriginal Desert art in its connection to other recent global histories of dispossession and cultural genocide.

This book explores the inspirational quality of Aboriginal acrylic art as it exceeds the markets. And it observes the *vivacity of images*, those of Western photojournalism no less than those of fine art or indigenous artifact, that take us beyond exchange.

From colonialism to the United Nations, from abstract expressionism to photojournalism, I cannot bring together the art and politics of this moment without grasping the dominant Western aesthetic of the Real World.

The Real World is a shopping mall, a conceptual space in which people and objects from different cultures encounter each other in such a way as to respond. But this response does not mean the same thing to each person involved. Different responses have different consequences for the viability of this space.

There are more and varied meanings in the plurality of postcolonial worlds than were previously imagined. Some of these meanings are misunderstood; some are contradictory. Some of them are incompatible with others, sometimes violently conflicting. Culture is now only observed in the plural, is only ever a comparative event.

And yet, at the same time, globalization imagines *one* world, a world of signs and indicators with universal translation. Many of these are economic.

The empirical sciences entail cultures of "realism" that permit the same interpretation across different worlds. This realism assumes a one-size-fits-all rationality that is most clearly articulated in international law, trade relations, and human rights.

I came to this conundrum through going shopping with Lily and Molly, Myra and Rosie; and more generally, through the case of Australian Aboriginal acrylic art. But it applies to many other kinds of sacred, many varieties of "indigenous," many different markets.

Through the specific case of Aboriginal painting, this book asks: How does the image today cultivate each of us to fit the Real World?

It matters at this moment in the study of indigenous art to focus on the operations of Western desire, on the "Western eye" that looks on the remarkable difference of this work as proof of its "cultural authenticity."

To quote Jim Clifford, we need to return to indigenous art objects "their lost status as *our* own fetishes," whose resistance to classification "could remind us of our lack of self-possession, of the artifices we employ to gather a world around us" (quoted in Myers, 2002:17).

It is not that the West cannot know the mystery of these works— that is the form of the fantasy itself, of a mystery that must necessarily be unknown. It is, rather, *what is known* by this art in its Western reception. It is the peculiar suitability of cultural difference for the category of mystery that emerges, strictly analogous with the mystery of nature and wilderness.

These mysteries come from the same place and time—the "Real World" of the twenty-first century, already technologized and rapidly globalizing. This is from where the echoes of other times and places are heard, as precious revenants, or as genuine gifts in an uneven exchange of ontologies.

In this book, I look at diverse figures: batik-making in adult education classes, the genesis of acrylic paints and the physiology of color; the violence of Australian "settler invasion" on the Aboriginal world and the assertion of law in painting; and abstract art and the mocking of the Western tradition in the artistic commodity.

These are all sacred exchanges. The sacred, as "being bearing meaning" (Kristeva and Clement, 2001), is one key to the production of value, as I hope this array will show. Art, through its access to the plasticity of aesthetic ordering, shows us that production in miniature, under laboratory conditions, inside a cordon sanitaire erected around it to protect it from becoming too real.

Utopia

Utopia is a desert community in outback Australia, renowned for a group of remarkable Aboriginal artists. The women from this station are especially known for their acrylic painting and their batik: names like Emily Kngwarreye, Kathleen Petyarre, Gloria Petyarre, Minnie Pwerle. Utopia is 240 kilometers northeast of Alice Springs, accessible only by four-wheel drive.

The name, Utopia, is apt, conveying the engagement of Aboriginal Dreamtime with a legendary aspirational space in European lore. *Utopia* captures the difference between European and Aboriginal notions of time and place. It renders the irony of Aboriginal life in postcolonial Australia, and the violence of European settlement that through malice and misadventure threatened to destroy Aboriginal cultures.

The story of how the Dreamings were revived and reinvented as icons on the international contemporary art scene is a utopic one in many ways. For some in the European world, it is indeed a utopia in which one *becomes* an artist in order to make a living. In 1994, as Vivien Johnson describes it:

In a population of seven hundred people, of whom more than half are young children, there are more than a hundred practising artists at Lajamanu, a statistic indicating a degree of artistic ferment that few places outside of New York could boast.

By the end of the 1980s, there was not a general store in any of the dozens of small communities dotted across the vast expanses of the Western Desert that did not stock paints and canvas to supply the local artists. (Johnson 1996: 41)

Every adult member of Western Desert Aboriginal society had a heritage of culture and training in the *jukurrpa* or Dreaming. This entitled them, as she observes, to embrace the vocation of artist: "and the way things were going, it looked as though they just might" (ibid.).

Dreaming

Kathleen Petyarre paints her *Mountain Devil Lizard* Dreaming canvases in a fine veil of dotting that resembles aerial photography of her Anankhere country. Christine Nicholls characterizes the presence of the Dreaming in Petyarre's canvases in this way: "Underneath the screen of Kathleen's very fine dotting the Dreaming exists as a barely tangible, shadowy palimpsest, overwritten, in effect, by the surface colours and movement" (Nichols and North, 2001:14).

But the English word *dreaming* is a poor translation of the Aboriginal concept that it attempts to name. Different words in different Aboriginal languages are called this Western state of unconsciousness: the Yolngu word *wangarr*, the Warlpiri *jukurrpa*, and the Arrernte (Aranda) *altyerrenge*. But Dreamings are not unconscious so much as a different kind of consciousness, a metaphysical apperception that permeates the physical world.

Spencer and Gillen first translated the Arrernte word as "Dreamtime" in 1896 (Morphy 1998:67–68). They justified this by noting the word *altyerrenge* was used of "events associated with ancestral beings in mythic times and to representations of those times." The word *alteyerra* was also the word used for "dream," and the suffix *—enge* signified possession: so, "Dreamtime" (ibid.).

But it would be wrong to see the word *Dreamtime* as a literal translation of an equivalent term in all Aboriginal languages. Some Aboriginal people dislike its connotation, since "the Dreaming" is "not a dream but a reality," as they put it (Morphy 1998:67–68). Unlike *altyerrenge*, the Yolngu word *wangarr*, from Arnhem land, cannot be translated literally as Dreamtime, and Yolngu feel the connotation of illusion demeans the place of *wangarr* in culture.

To speak of Petyarre's canvases as representing Dreaming stories forecloses questions that Aboriginal philosophies open in suggestive ways. Morphy has argued: "The concept of the Dreaming, a uniquely Aboriginal way of placing people in time and space, forces one to think differently, and in a less linear way, about the relationship between form and creativity in art" (1998:4).

Western understandings separate the subject from its objects, but Aboriginal Dreamings appear not to work like this. I say "appear" because I am acutely aware that, my thought having been given to me via the categories of Western life, I am unlikely ever to inhabit a world in which I am *not* separated from my objects by my thought. This is a condition of my Western subjectivity, and thereby of my ontology.

Nevertheless, I am familiar with objects that complicate this view, even in the Real World. The leading example would be my body, which (borrowing the sentiment from Valéry) belongs to me a little less than I belong to it. I can imagine the possibility of inhabiting the world differently when I experience the heat of a desert day, for example. Traveling in the outback, "going out to country," involves a physical immersion that I cannot comprehend merely by viewing a map.

"Country" is a translation of an Aboriginal concept much larger than nature, land, or place. It is enriched with both archetypal and social meanings, and imbued also with the deep sense of belonging that knowledge

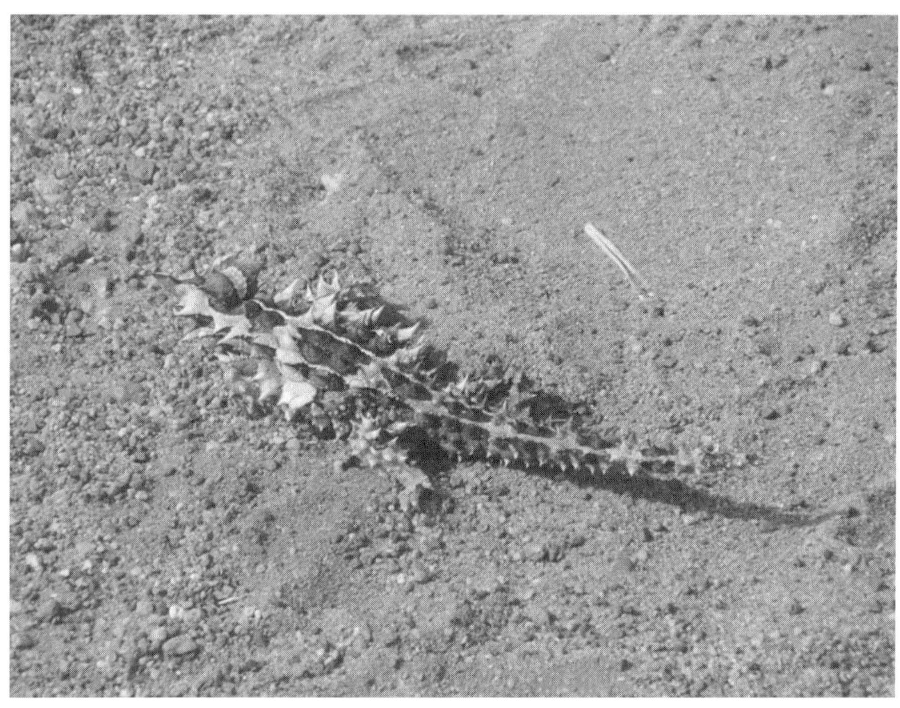

of the Dreamings conveys. Rosalyn Diprose writes of this Indigenous philosophy in terms of the closest Western analogue, contemporary work in the phenomenological tradition. Emphasizing the aspects of subjective perception that underscore our own knowledge (in this, drawing especially on the thought of Merleau-Ponty), she observes: "Where I see footprints in sand Kathleen Petyarre sees the mountain devil lizard, the mountain devil lizard Dreaming carving up the dirt and creating a world of meaning as it wanders through the land" (2006:33).

> According to her authorised spokesperson, Christine Nicholls, Petyarre makes a direct correlation between her navigation of the landscape with her family through childhood, and her expression of the landscape of the Dreaming in painting [Diprose 2006: 38]. Nicholls suggests that the artistic expression of Petyarre's spatial knowledge of the landscape is due to an "ability to reconstruct, from memory, detailed and accurate mental maps" of the terrain of her childhood [Nicholls and North 2001:7], so accurate that her canvasses of the landscape bear a remarkable resemblance to aerial photographs of the terrain [Ibid.].

The phenomenological understanding that Diprose details allows for another inflection. She suggests that Petyarre's expression of the Dreaming is not a mental map, but rather a transformed echo of her bodily orientation toward, and expression of, country. "Through her inheritance of meaning of the Dreaming through dwelling with the elders and through her simultaneous bodily navigation of the land, Petyarre has herself become the mountain devil lizard dreaming."

Through the concept of dreams, of course, I can capture a sense in which the world is experienced differently. Whitefellas dream, too, and some are troubled by their dreaming. Dream states are not commonly regarded as a kind of thought in Western culture. Yet a tradition of valuing the insights of dreams can be found; in *The Interpretation of Dreams* (1900), Freud goes so far as to map the rhetoric of the dream as a meaningful but encrypted style of thought.

Perhaps the salient aspect of the psychoanalytic understanding of dreaming for appreciation of the Aboriginal Dreaming is the way in which the material world of objects and events is invested with meanings for the dreamer, as expressions of desires and fears. But there is no need to turn to psychology to find the deep intelligence of this reflection, since the artistic genres themselves carry that necessity. Dance and drama, music and architecture all require a different mode of interpretation from a literal text or a realistic image.

"Spencer and Gillen's photographs of ceremonies in Central Australia show just how transforming the body art of Australia is, and how easy it is to imagine that the dancers are manifestations of the ancestral beings as they were when they emerged from the earth" (Morphy 1998:91). The character of these beings "is almost ineffable, grasped only for the moment. In their most concrete form they can be seen embodied in the form of the landscape and in the birth of a child, but the ancestor moves on and the child grows old and dies. They exist, in essence, as an idea, as a creative force that touches many different things and appears in many different manifestations, but which cannot be reduced to any one of them. It may be for this reason that ancestral beings are often portrayed not so much by figurative representations of objects that occur in the natural world as by more abstract geometric forms" (ibid.).

This seems to describe an *aesthetic*. The Dreaming emerges as an ordering of sensations and impressions into a scene that "makes sense." It does so as a living practice.

As Jennifer Biddle points out, "even the most sympathetic accounts of Petyarre's work, … juxtapose canvasses of Petyarre's with representations of the 'real': cartographic maps, 'iconic' translations; photographs of red country and mountain devils" (2006:61). While acknowledging the political salience of these cultural keys, Biddle argues that the effect of the "generic" Dreamings of Petyarre's later work (and of other Utopia artists such as Emily Kngwarreye) is to insist "on the productivity of painting itself as an autonomous materiality" (ibid.:63).

These works, she writes, "bring the Dreaming into being. Ancestral potency arises within these paintings and is actively produced by them. . . . This textuality does not point or defer. The energy emanating from these works is inescapably immediate. Viscerally-charged and haptically exuberant, Petyarre's work is above all else, *affective*. These paintings incite and excite" (ibid.:64).

The challenge presented by the Dreaming is not one of a mysticism opposed to a social history. Writes Morphy: "The recent history of Aboriginal art has been a dialogue with colonial history" (1998:4).

As Morphy has said of the acrylic art: "The paintings missed out the stage of being primitive art altogether and became almost overnight part of Australian contemporary art" (ibid.:315). "Batik designs were part of Emily Kame Kngwarreye's heritage as much as the body designs that influenced her later paintings. Western Desert art . . . is a dialogue between the present and the past in the context of the ever widening world in which people live" (ibid.:316).

Aboriginal graphic displays are "embedded in ritual and ceremonial activities which are in many senses economic exchanges" (Michaels 1987:138). "Designs signify, among other things, rights: to songs; to myths; and to the land and its resources that they depict and celebrate." Petyarre's art is formed inside the European art scene, as much a product of it as of the Dreaming. The synthesis of Aboriginal Dreaming practices with European "economic realities" is the genius of Aboriginal acrylic art.

Petyarre is steeped in the law of Anankherre Dreaming, but lives sometimes in suburban Adelaide. Emily Kame Kngwarreye had a similarly traditional education, but became a modernist celebrity in her last years. They demonstrate this synthesis, by picking up the threads of the Dreaming law in the means offered desert communities for economic survival—batik painting, and later, painting with acrylics on canvas.

Kngwarreye's and Petyarre's paintings are precisely not "painting traditional Aboriginal designs," but enact an aesthetic of the impossible

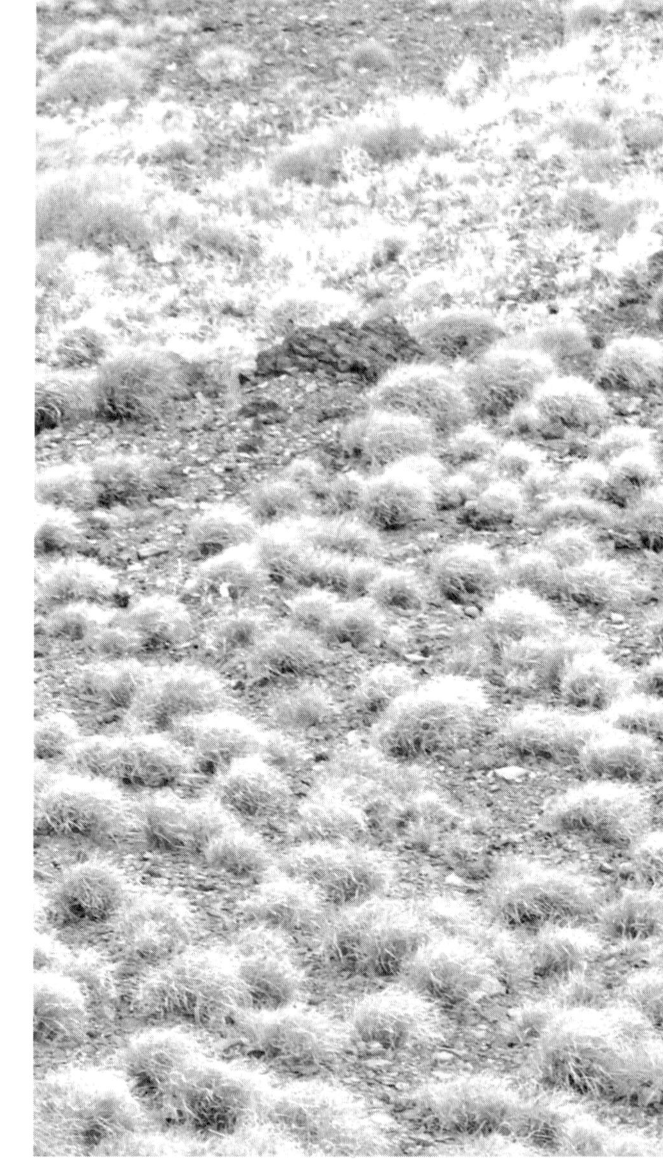

collision of Aboriginal and European worlds in the artists' time and place. These canvases are new Dreamings, sensations of contact with Western orderings that provide a rich artistic provocation in the work.

Desert painting generally represents the adaptation of Aboriginal culture to meet the Western world view: the transposition of sand and body painting from the ground of ceremony to the picture plane of canvas and acrylic paint. The Western Desert acrylic art became the first Aboriginal art to be recognized alongside other Australian art as a serious, contemporary event of style.

Its acceptance is partly due "to the art's remarkable similarities to modern Western abstract painting" (Sutton 1988:90). The ontology of signs is expressed in the art—"the Aboriginal artist generally seeks to create reductive *signs for* the things represented" (ibid.:37, author's emphasis)—which is thereby "conceptual" rather than "perceptual," as much writing as painting. In the iconography, the sacred meanings of the world can be both displayed and encrypted. The status of Aboriginal art as "an iconic religious form of landscape art" (ibid.:81) links it to a visual logic that Western eyes have been prepared for.

Questions of belief and truth are also meaningful for modern Western abstract art. But there are some ways in which the Desert paintings—the ontology of the Dreaming that it expresses—maintain a perplexing distance from the postmodern. This is shown, for example, in the deceptively simple exclamation made by Sutton's Aboriginal friend: "The land *is* a map!" he says (Sutton 1998:19).

The stories of the Dreamings are as close to law and theology as they are to the poetic; they express a deep epistemic relation to the land that in traditional life created both social structure and legal entitlements. The painted expression of Dreamings does not decorate, but rather mobilizes, a realm of intelligibility that produced the Aboriginal world.

As Eric Michaels has written (specifically of the Yuendumu art), "These paintings make the claim that the landscape does speak and that it speaks directly to the initiated, and explains not only its own occurrence, but the order of the world" (1987:143).

There is something fortuitous in the Desert art "looking like" abstract art, "modern art," at the same time as it arises under and gains its celebrity in the genre of "indigenous art," which is precisely *not* modern, as far as the map of the artwork commodity goes. That fortuity tells us something important about the creation and reception of art, as it does about the creation and reception of political categories like "indigenous."

It is fortuitous that this interest meets in Desert painting, whose works show the scars of Indigenous contact with European culture, at just that time when these two categories might be said to have *unsettled* each other. Not that the exchange was ever equal, but there was finally beginning to be an exchange, where there had previously been nothing but the imperious exercise of exclusion (art versus artifact, civilized versus "primitive" where "primitive" belongs to that Eurocentric discussion in which Western artists were measuring themselves, initiated versus uninitiated, art theory versus ethnography).

This fortuity is intensified by Kngwarreye, Petyarre, and others also entering into the category of "woman artist," since that celebrity itself has unsettled the traditional categories of "the artist" and "artistic genius," as it has confronted "traditional art" (Battersby 1989). An indigenous woman artist painting very large abstract canvases might be an important incongruity.

So, an indigenous art and a feminist politics, indigenous politics and feminist aesthetics, collide in the placement of this work and its viewers now. Moreover, these spheres collide *in the work itself.*

It might be held that the lack of figuration in their recent work has nothing to do with the moving beyond figuration that just happens to coincide with it in modern art. To understand this fortuity as more than a superficial—even cynical, albeit profitable—error of appreciation, one needs better to understand what it might mean to experience cross-cultural exchange and what it would be to appreciate a work of art.

Abstraction

The canvases of Abstract Expressionists like Mark Rothko belong at the forefront of what it is to paint "abstractly" in the cultural imagination. Rothko's milieu is still adjacent to the contemporary: the work does not look "old"—but all the same, it looks like "fine art."

Further, Rothko's painting still exercises a fascination over respectable criticism as well as over populist blurb. Rothko attracts the piety of high art appreciation—a seriousness that may be deserved but that is not accorded to every art historical moment. Indeed, Rothko may stand as the epiphany of Western abstraction because of his "imageless images," fields of color that assert only a "logic of sensation" (Deleuze 2003).

The preoccupation in Western contemporary art with itself grows out of the metaphysical consequences of a loss of meaning. It is hard not to ally this with the narcissism of colonialism, which by the middle of the twentieth century, when Abstract Expressionism became an identifiable movement, was a view of the world coming under increasing pressure.

The Abstract Expressionists were familiar with the "primitive" art available to New York buyers at that time. They, like other European artists such as Picasso, saw aesthetic value in it and admired it by emulating it. But the difference between what they were doing with these motifs and what earlier artists had done, as they saw it, was immense.

Whereas styles and figures were adopted to decorative effect by many artists, the Abstract Expressionists imagined *they painted from the same place*— that they respected, and moreover shared, the spiritual mission of the indigenous artist. In a manifesto, Gottlieb and Rothko declare, against a formal notion of abstraction, that "the subject is crucial and only that subject matter is valid which is tragic and timeless. That is why we profess spiritual kinship with primitive and archaic art" (Tate Gallery 1987:77–78).

But are the Dreamings "tragic and timeless," according to this imagined affinity with them? The translation of the Dreamings from the sand

and the body to the picture plane has metaphysical consequences—it reveals the potential of these marks to become *abstract*. Where they may have been lived—imbibed through the treading out of the ground in ceremony, or wedded to the skin—on canvas the design can be visualized and scrutinized. Perhaps an epistemological crisis starts here; the virtual is opened, and with it the prospect of simulacrum; the assertion of title to country is raised simultaneously in its dispossession.

Or are these works, on the contrary, *free* of the transcendental? Revealed as a painting event that, like ceremonies and other cultural "business," occurs *every time* in time and space, as familial, economic, and without irony even in its forced encounter with the picture plane?

Is the Abstract Expressionists' claim to "spiritual kinship" merely a Western avarice-nostalgia for forms of society that never were, a colonial privilege that came complete with the Jungian warrant to raid a collective unconscious and assume title to *every* culture?

Aboriginal artists would be unlikely to corroborate the claim to kinship. *Their* abstraction lays claim to title to country—being able to make the marks shows knowledge of a law whose provenance is given by the ability of the initiated to paint it. Painting is a claim, but its entitlement is an *effect of the artist's embodiment*, not of his or her appropriation.

Terry Smith speaks of a transformation of the whole task of the interpreter of the abstract, brought on by Aboriginal artforms, toward "a struggle to grasp what its template was; that is, what it began from as a representation." He reflects on the resulting thought of painting as "the space [that] came into being in the making of the mark itself" (Smith 2006:36).

But abstraction in twentieth-century art theory develops a grandiloquent narrative about the end of art, which ends in adopting abstraction as the metaphor for intelligibility and the crisis of meaning. These modernist views of abstraction have in turn been challenged in postmodernism; John Rachjman refers us to Deleuze's "logic of sensation," in which abstraction emerges as a possibility that must be "rethought along several lines at once."

The gross exclusive opposition between figurative and abstract loses its centrality, and a good deal of its interest, in favour of kinds of pictorial space, and the kinds of figurability they permit. For images or figures are not created out of nothing to match with external models; they "come into being" from a compositional space which always departs from visual coordinates, creating strange new sensations. Abstraction is thus not in the first instance to be understood as the emptying of illusionist space of figures and stories; it is, rather, a sort of "sensation" of this other larger sort of abstract space which precedes and exceeds it. (Rachjman 1995:21)

This seems to fit the case of Desert painting well. To understand these canvases as abstract in this sense would be to understand them to be initiating the meeting of European and Aboriginal as a kind of painting. The paintings in their different projections of pictorial space can resuscitate the figurable from a crisis in which it could be said to have been unrepresentable, irresolvable. The crisis is, literally, a "conflict of laws"; Aboriginal law in contest with English common law, which has subjugated but not annihilated it.

Rachjman argues that chance is the essence of the abstract. In the fortuity of Desert painting, its coincidental "looking-like" is a coincidence occurring in "irreversible time." It is chance originating not as probability but as irrevocability. The "chance" effects of individual canvases—effects that are not by any means accidental, nor are they accomplished by chance, in that they require a high degree of technical control to execute—speak directly to the process by which Aboriginal life has been irrevocably altered through the violent encounter with the colonial.

Striking Color

Painting with acrylics on canvas has not only brought abstraction, it has brought with it an "explosion" of color, into Desert art. It defies, as Judith

Ryan notes, "mythical preconceptions that the quintessential colors of Aboriginal art are natural ochres" (2004: 98).

Ryan likens it to the impact of Fauvism on the evolution of Modernism in early twentieth-century Europe. And the importance of the color in Desert art takes place in this context, challenging further the distinction between "primitive" and "modern." The challenge is to elucidate the context.

The contagion of color in Aboriginal art is more than a happy accident. The romantic assumption that the old artists are untouched by modern banalities such as air travel and magazines, and that even if known to them, these visualizations would be alien to "their culture," is as naïve as it is patronizing. Outback Aboriginal communities are deprived in many ways, but not of the mass media images that enculture us all.

You can watch television in the outback (CAAMA, the Central Australian Aboriginal Media Association, has been making Aboriginal content since the late 1970s); there are weekly scheduled commercial flights into the Western Desert. You can buy a copy of *Women's Weekly* and *TV Times* at roadhouses on the Stuart Highway. The clinic and the church disseminate their own versions of modern life in pamphlets; the school art room has poster paint along with views on what a painting ought to look like.

Traditionally, Aboriginal people produced pigments and tints from plants, seeds, and rocks, which they also traded with other groups. But the use of the full range of the acrylic palette, which is itself the material of an industrial chemistry and history, signs up to the Western history of color, whether artists know it, intend it, or desire it. Which only goes to show that in this respect Aboriginal artists do not differ from other artists who are directed by the manufacturing process, and given many of their possibilities through the modern manner of providing materials, in tubes or bottles from art suppliers.

Color has always carried its material meanings. In the time of the guilds, European artists used "ultramarine" on the robe of the Virgin and the patron where it could signify precedence, since being made from lapis lazuli it was a costly pigment. Diane Young observes that the seasonal colors used in some painting by Mutijulu women signify temporality. Eric Michaels notes the Karrku red, named after Mt. Karrku, where the ochre is found, can carry a reference to this country in Warlpiri work. And Yves Klein famously patented various blues, imbuing them with property, as well as color, values.

The pleasure of color has been cultivated for the contemporary viewer by a rich engagement with it by artists over a century of modern art. Color has its theory from Kandinsky, Mondrian, and Matisse to Klein, Hodgkins, Rothko, and Agnes Martin. I may know nothing of this and yet still succumb to the historical effect when I see on the canvas what was put there for me to find.

Historical survey seems to show no unanimity across cultures on how many, and which, of the colors are primary. Color theories abound, from the four-colored palette of the Greeks to the "color without theory" empiricism of the twentieth century. In John Gage's engrossing study of color and culture, a history is given of these changes in views on color and how they have been influenced by both the theoretical and practical concerns of artists, scientists, and philosophers.

The development of a chromatic idiom belonging to the West, and indeed to contemporary Western art, attests not to essential color qualities but to a thoroughly contextualized sense of "hue" in any culture. Experimental psychology fails to demonstrate a universal symbolic scheme for colors, but hue and tone, like timbre and tonality, develop, through bodily experience, into systems "like a language" in a structuralist sense.

Color evolved metaphysical alliances, commonly contrasted with line, design, or form. This distinction refers back to Aristotle's between form and matter. Traditionally, the vivacity of *colore* can obscure the *disegno*, generating tension between the recognition of color's capacity to flesh out the artist's idea or usurp it.

In the West, the feelings of color, like other feelings, have long been given to women: to wear and otherwise to embody as visual signs of desire. So color has commonly been associated with the feminine in art history. The relationship between *disegno* and *colore* as one of gendered opposition originates in antiquity.

There is evidence that color is the innovation of Desert women's art in particular. Whether by its different lineage as tourist art or from the lesser attention initially paid to the women's painting as fine art, the color of canvases like Eubena Nampitjin, Makinti Napanangka, or Judy Watson slips into an associative train of thought already anticipated in the Western viewer, although it may be unrelated to gender distinction in Aboriginal lore.

In the twentieth century, many Western artists experimented with color as a way of expressing the experience of looking. Merleau-Ponty tells us that "Cézanne abandons two-dimensional perspective for a whole period of his career because he seeks expression through color." And, following Cézanne, one can think of Delaunay, Rothko, Chagall, and Bacon, to name just a few, for whom color was a characteristic approach to the visual.

Art movements like surrealism, cubism, and modernism challenged the self-evidence of the senses, and color played its part in this.

The limit of color as a compositional element may have been reached with the "color without theory" practitioners, who replace shape and figure in composition with color, as a route to abstraction. More than this, it emerged as *abstraction itself*, and expressing the same paradox as Clement Greenberg noted for abstraction: "Something given independent of meanings, similars or originals; content is to be dissolved so completely into form that the work of art cannot be reduced to anything not itself" (quoted in Harrison and Wood 2003).

Color as abstraction had self-reference in terms of the autonomy that Greenberg outlines, but also expressed a salutary self-absorption, in creating pure painterly expressivity on a material plane. Color was abstraction's element, at least as painting; the possibility of both substance and form. As Matisse described it:

> That effect of color has real power. . . . So much power that, in certain lights, it seems to become a substance. Once when I found myself in the chapel, I saw on the ground a red of such materiality that I had the feeling that the color was not the effect of light falling through the window, but that it belonged to some substance. This impression was reinforced by a particular circumstance: on the floor in front of me there was some sand in a little pile that the red color was resting on. That gave me the effect of red powder so magnificent that I have never seen the like in my life. (quoted in Gage 1993:212)

In Albers's *Homage to a Square* or Noland's stripes, the attempt was made to neutralize form in favor of the pure material of color. But Gage argues they were only partly successful, in that the contribution to the *color* relations on the plane made by the shape of the stripe, square, or chevron was overlooked. "The regular repeats and hard edges of this motif inevitably affect our perception of the colors by simultaneous and successive contrast; and this ultimate coloristic style of painting shows us that, as in the past, color and form are inseparable" (1993:256).

The growth in interest in color as substance also came from the direction of science, as empirical psychology and industrial chemistry. "Color without theory" resisted this proliferating scientific and critical color theory with the attitude that, in painting, color belonged not to the scientist but to the artist. Ironically, this attitude was described as "empiricist." The intuition was that "painting by eye," like playing by ear, was properly artistic, and that color application need not be directed by exterior ideology. As Frank Stella declared, "Thinking about color abstractly hasn't done me any good" (Gage 1993:268).

An ironic reversal in the *colore-disegno* opposition is seen in the production of works from the Kimberley region in Western Australia, where

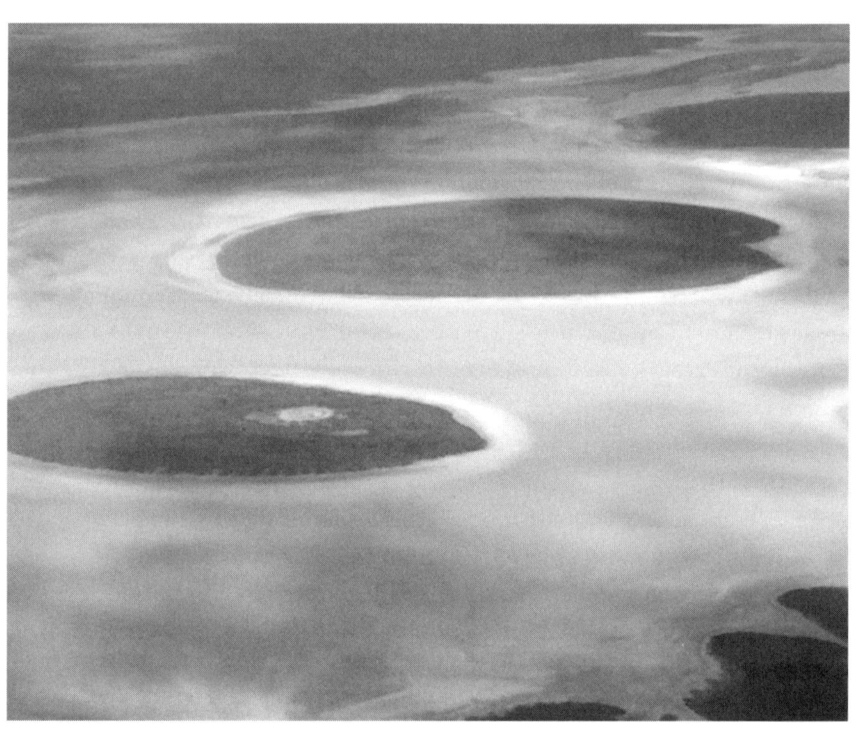

artists like Paddy Bedford, Freddy Timms, and Rover Thomas use traditional ochres *as if* they were acrylic paint. In the giant color fields of a Freddy Timms, for example, the abstraction refers to contemporary art while it is the color itself, the ochres of the region, that references country. The *colore* carries forward an Indigenous past, while *disegno* cries out to the contemporary Western moment.

This is a highly complex gesture, politically and aesthetically. It conveys the paradox of a continuing practice of the Dreaming, in which postinvasion events like the Bedford Downs and Ruby Plains massacres enter into ceremony alongside older stories of country. The production of this art as large-scale, museum-quality canvases aimed at the high end of the contemporary art market commands political as well as artistic credibility for the Aboriginal postcolonial experience.

The Real Power of Color

"Blue is that which prompts me to look in a certain way, that which allows my gaze to run over it in a specific manner. It is a certain field or atmosphere presented to the power of my eyes and of my whole body." (Merleau-Ponty 1962: 210)

Although we can measure colors as particular wavelengths of light, this does not completely capture the experience of them, and it cannot tell their whole story (as the long debate on color in philosophy attests). The sensation of blue is not just knowledge of a certain standard or convention. This is because color is an interaction between the body and the world. Seeing colors depends not only on the wave-lengths of light (which follow the spectrum) but also on the absorbing properties of the surface, the light in which something is viewed, and the context of other colored shapes around it. Not only physicists but artists, photographers, and industrial chemists are familiar with the paradoxical effects of color. Merleau-Ponty discusses experiments that suggest colors cause us to respond with muscular action (moving toward red, away from blue) even before we have registered what we are looking at. Some have been tempted to declare fundamental universals in color and its effects, but John Gage, in his survey *Color and Meaning*, demonstrates the variety of color ideas in history, and hence the significance of context. As his last chapter on synaesthesia research suggests, this contextual sensitivity extends beyond the borders of "ideas" into our bodies as cultural products. "The history of synaesthesia suggests that the very senses themselves, which have generally been thought of as bodily functions, are not exempt from, or are by and large the products of, cultural conditioning" (1999:268).

The astounding directness of Desert art can be attributed partly to its strong color effects. But if color ideas are contextual, then how are they also communicative across cultures, so as to make this art, composed from an esoteric sacred knowledge, delight the Western eye?

Research with aphasics has shown that color has an effect on the nervous system before it is perceived cognitively: "I clenched my teeth, so I know that it is yellow" (Merleau-Ponty 1962:211). At the same time, Gage acknowledges that association, especially word association, also plays a part in the observed effects of color, at least for European subjects.

An example of this from the history of Desert art is striking; the "earth" palette adopted earlier in the movement (probably on the initiative of art advisers of the day) served to signify the art as "primitive" in the 1970s, even if it also referenced the real context of ochres, sand, and charcoal.

Conversely, the exuberant mauves, scarlets, blues, and oranges of the more recent Aboriginal acrylics signify something contemporary, and indeed the pleasurable contradiction of a "modern primitive" art. Part of the excitement generated by this art is this juxtaposition, suggestive of cultural resilience, and even of the renaissance of tribal identity in a world beguiled by this possibility.

The affective movements solicited by color are highly valued in the Real World. Through advertising, commercial art, and couture, we are trained in color affects but usually only subliminally. Without a language for them, we are only affected.

Color can take us back to the precognitive and even the preperceptual, to an archaic layer of sensation readily associated with the oceanic, the prelinguistic and the maternal. By this route, color becomes a vehicle for the spiritual. Without a plausible language of the spirit in the Real World, bodily responses including affects are more mysterious, and indeed come to signal the *place* of mystery. This materialism is the sacred of the Western modern.

Sensory animation is an important consolation in this embodiment. The preperceptual effects of color become generalized to the whole aesthetic effect. Working from Francis Bacon's wish that his art should "work directly on the nervous system," Deleuze elaborates this aesthetic effect as a "logic of sensation" (2003, 36).

The color effects in Desert art work not so much to convey an understanding of the Dreaming as to animate an experience of the sacred. This may be why the art is so successful across cultures: the art *is* sacred, since it produces an auratic domain. And these effects, felt as sensations, deepen into political conviction. Fred Myers comments, in *Painting Culture: The Making of an Aboriginal High Art*:

"I understood what the painters said, of course, but I would never have anticipated the effects they had in producing a recognition of their value and power across cultural boundaries. They have contributed to the accomplishment of land tenure security, of establishing a significant identity for those whose Dreamings they are, and they have made a kind of aboriginality knowable to those who view them. In this way, they have evidenced the power they were said to have" (2002:361).

How Painting Began

Before Emily Kngwarreye began painting, she had been introduced, like other desert women, to the craft of batik-printing on fabric. The traditional designs work well on cloth, and the innovation of using wax with a paintbrush, as the Utopia artists did, created a distinctive effect.

This was as part of adult education classes held across Australia in the 1970s. The enthusiasm for batik was not restricted to Indigenous communities, but passed through community centers, holiday camps, nursing homes, and schools like a willy-willy, or desert wind, accompanied by tie-dyeing and candlemaking for all.

It might be thought that this engagement of Central Desert art with batik-painting was an encounter with another "indigenous" craft tradition. Batik was customary to Indonesian groups, who used the technique of dripping wax as a resist onto cloth and then dyeing it. It began as an anthropological curiosity, like other artifacts in the colonial world. But it was not as a cross-cultural exchange of scholarly self-consciousness that batik came to be made in the Australian desert.

Balinese batik came back to Australia as the ubiquitous shirt or sarong in the 1970s, on the back of the developing tourist trade. Like package holidays, the adult education classes that taught batik-making were not about high art, but the commodity of "leisure," sold in digestible time-slices to an increasingly prosperous middle Australia.

Adult education was not about democratizing anthropology, and batik-making had no designs on producing fine art. The activities of tourism and art classes were aimed at consumers, not producers, as ways to stave off aimlessness and to fill in the time that was not commandeered to productive or reproductive labor, or consumption.

Examples of the batik cloth made by Central Desert women artists are now held in the collection of public galleries and displayed as one moment in the art history of the movement (for example, National Gallery of Victoria 2008). Likewise, Balinese theater and design have also become the subject of ethnographic reflection—for example, in the interest shown in the *gamelan* orchestra in contemporary cultural studies.

But the claim that "batik emerged as a dynamic new form of Aboriginal art during the 1970s and 1980s" (National Gallery of Victoria 2008) is made with the benefit of hindsight. At the time, the naïveté of adult

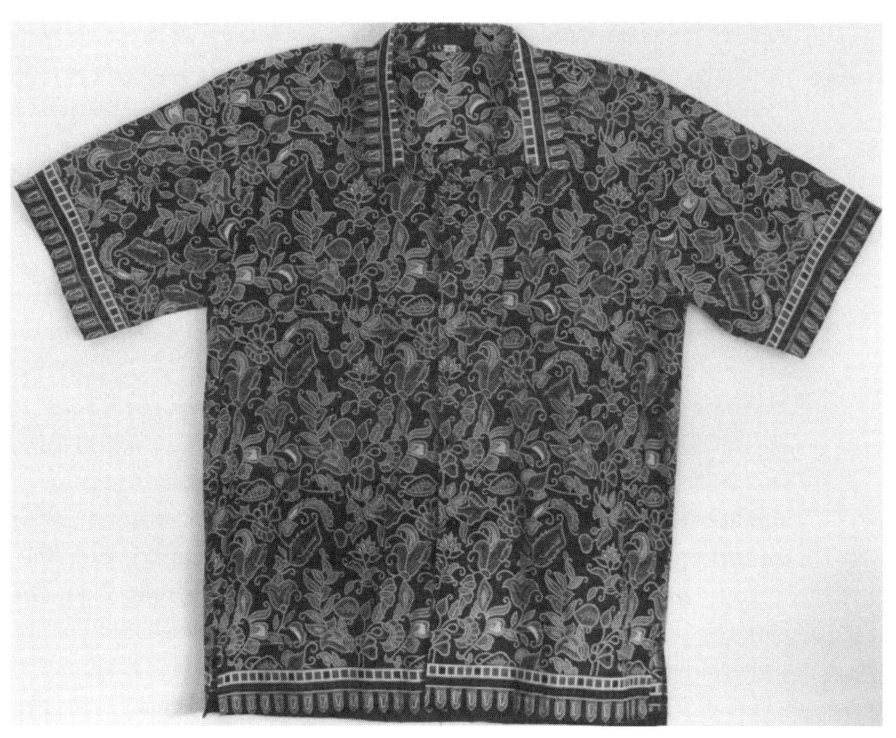

education was only one of the many historical "accidents" that have been productive in the making of Aboriginal art. In *Papunya Painting: Out of the Desert*, John Kean, involved in the early days of Papunya Tula, the first painting mob, deals optimistically and not euphemistically (as is the trend in the market) with the ways in which the evolving of a style was not so obviously a destiny at the time. The works "were often painted in confusing circumstances permeated by cultural misunderstanding. None of us who were involved in the painting movement at that time could have known the influence that these paintings would go on to have" (Johnson 2007:15).

And Vivien Johnson comments on genuinely material effects directing the development of the art, for example, of the available canvas sizes, and gallery protocols for palette and scale. "The idea of trying canvas as an alternative arose from logistical shipping considerations, but its introduction had far-reaching artistic consequences" (Johnson 2007:31).

Aboriginal acrylic painting "began" at Papunya with the *Honey Ant Dreaming* mural, as a rebel act by Pintupi male elders desperate to protect their country and driven to put aside the secrecy of law to do so.

Geoff Bardon gives an account of the beginning of the painting style, as the whitefella mentor who assisted it, in *Papunya: A Place Made after the Story* (2004). His engagement with Aboriginal designs started with the children, since he was the art teacher at the settlement school. Using litho paper and powdered poster paint mixed with PVA glue, he tells of encouraging the children to express their own stories. There was an availablitiy of these basic materials at Papunya, strangely enough, considering the absences of other basics of life, such as shelter and cash.

It matters perhaps that the way toward a humane possibility in the space between Aboriginal and European cultures opened through the school. The same was seen later in the painting of *Yuendumu Doors* at the school in Yuendumu, and from the same impulse—to communicate, to a generation that had never known it in its traditional iteration, the cultural bond of country (Michaels 1987).

From his account, it seems that Bardon first understood himself to be offering the balm of creative expression to a group of men whose self-respect was being damaged by the circumstances of settlement. Bardon provided them with a means to communicate their own estimation of themselves—a radical gesture from the European toward the Aboriginal, yet the stock-in-trade of the art teacher toward his or her students.

The result was incidentally "landscape painting" and "sacred art." It would be just as legible today as "art therapy" or a community art initia tive. Bardon taught the Aboriginal artists as he would no doubt have taught other art students, to work up their own visual language. They responded so remarkably that he must have been highly gratified. He showed them the possibilities of painting on boards and canvases, engaging their visuality with the picture plane.

It was from here that the students taught the teacher—demonstrating how capably they already imagined "in abstract," in *abstraction*, having got hold of the surface as the kind of projection they were accustomed to making in other media like ceremony, dance, and song. They produced, as Bardon described it, "aphorisms of space."

The canvas became a rendering of a hypothesis, an idea or "diagram," to adopt Deleuze's terms (2003). But the artists had no need of Deleuze—their metaphysical capacities came from a quite other tradition, from the *observation* of difference and repetition, and the virtues of translating between genres, from image to story, and between dimensions, from space (design) to time (ceremony).

Bardon supplied the materials for this enterprise—the paints and the surfaces—and in doing so, he provided its terms. They were realistic terms, because they allowed the painters to come together as artists, to form a school and then a movement, predicated on making visible the kinds of Aboriginal expressions that remained vivacious enough to inspire, even despite the earlier history of attempts to subdue them.

But Bardon's terms made the movement a renaissance of sensibility, not a revival of a "primitive art." Its "high art" potential developed from its neologism: Western art materials, new visual languages, renderings on and of the picture plane. In particular, the style was uniquely fitted for the new materials of acrylic paints. These plastic, synthetic, ultramodern media were first made available to fine art painters in 1963 in the United Kingdom; Howard Hodgkin and David Hockney were making acrylics acceptable to the fine art market when the Australian Aboriginal painters were introduced to them.

Acrylic was a medium belonging to the commercial art world; to the world of synthetic polymers and industrial chemistry, to the worlds of cheap, durable student art supplies, suitable for mass distribution. This paint had the right kind of genius to parallel the Desert art movement. It could adapt a view of the Australian landscape to hyperreal color, evoking the phenomenology of the desert country and accentuating the non-realist visions of its spare but extraordinary landforms like Uluru, the Macdonnell ranges, the saltpans of Lake Mackay. Its plastic possibilities—quick drying, malleable, water based—could form a painting practice for the Desert painters where conditions made more traditional fine art media, like oils, unsuitable.

Albert Namatjira had painted in watercolor. As a colorist he cannot be faulted, but it is evident that the dominant techniques of washes and sketches did not lend themselves to breaking away from the compulsory realist perspective that dominated Australian landscape art. And oil paint, the currency of Western fine art, dried too slowly for use in a bush camp, where painting is done on the ground among the dust, the kids, and the dogs. The application of oils needs to be elaborate and specialized in order to achieve satisfying results. It is also expensive. In short, oil paint was a material for the *cognoscenti*.

Acrylic could cue "art education," but it might also cue "contemporary art." The special resonances of this new material collaborated with the new artists in a rich and surprising way, making possible a new genre.

To code Desert art as "authentic culturally" is a fetishizing of what is nevertheless a unique self-assertion of cultural sensibility. The dreary earth palette of "authenticity" might obscure the violence of colonization, cover over the way *this* art movement sprang from a time when these tribal people were forced into camps likened to penal or concentration camps, for the stated purpose of cutting off their traditional ways of life.

And while the terms of this self-assertion involved the commodification of the art market, and the adoption of Western art practices of visualization and materials, it was all the same a *production* of value, and not a simulation of it.

Papunya: A Place Made after the Story conjures the conditions of the Papunya camps in the early 1970s as violent and terrible, places of de facto imprisonment and subjugation.

There were vicious fights among the various tribal groups, and the enforced stay and attendant idleness at the camps and absence of game nearby were only the beginnings of the terrible enemy of all the people: drunkenness … which could rage through the camps like a fire day and night, and seemed to incite many men and women to a particularly terrifying violence.… Packs of dogs, both owned and unattached, roamed the dusty tracks and there were appalling diseases such as hepatitis and meningitis from which many children died; from your flat at night you would sometimes hear the screams and lamentations of the old or young, dying or being mourned, among the myriad star-like fires of Papunya glade, and I must say it was a strange and often terrible world. The people of the Welfare Branch said to me so often that I beheld a living museum, and an overarching thought among the teachers and administration was that not only Aboriginal culture but the Aboriginals themselves were set in a death-mould and that nothing in this world would save them.… As the red dust blew along the tracks of this death's mask of a settlement, death was always in your waking dreams. (Bardon 2004:8)

Those who deny that cultural genocide was taking place in the "assimilationist" policies and practices of the 1950s–1970s need to consider

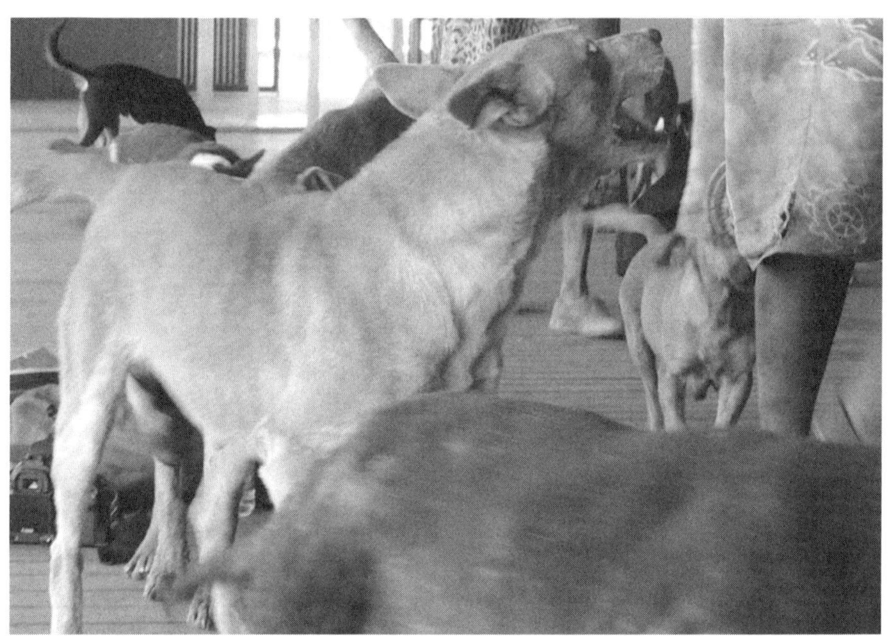

the similarities between Papunya and the work camps of Nazi Germany or the Stalinist gulags. There was a clear intent, in the policy that rounded up these people on the basis of ethnicity, and left them far from home in hostile country without meaningful employment, income, community, or assistance, to make their cultural survival highly unlikely.

What Bardon's story also emphasizes is the tremendous stirring that coming together to paint the *Honey Ant* mural became for the Pintupi. For them—but also for himself—it had the proportions of a renaissance.

His poetic narrative highlights the way in which the revivification of the designs was a rediscovery of culture, and of cultural pride, too. There is no doubting the critical importance this had for desert people, who were little better than interns at Papunya at the time.

Bardon paints his own picture, of racial hatred in the camps, in the disturbing accounts of the behavior of administrators toward their charges. Yet Papunya Tula remains today, in its durability, a touchstone for Aboriginal communities. "The term 'title deed' perfectly sums up mid- to late 1970s painting" (Johnson 2007:32) and many Aboriginal groups have followed, being able to reference their ownership of country through the knowledge of these designs. Stories of Papunya's enduring emphasize the speculation of its venture throughout the 1980s, by no means the accomplished fact it now in hindsight appears. All of this makes the way it finished up for Bardon sadder—by 1972, he left Papunya a broken man, under the pressure of white obstruction and black mistrust. His departure left behind the question, could anything have been done in that corrupted space that was not tainted with the racism, colonialism, contempt, and avarice that dominated the European action in relation to Aborigines? Could there have been an altruistic gesture by a white man? Or was Bardon's assistance in the production of Desert art the next step in colonizing, taking the culture, too?

It has been remarked that the resistance to the revealing of traditional law, by other groups like the Warlpiri language group (one of the largest

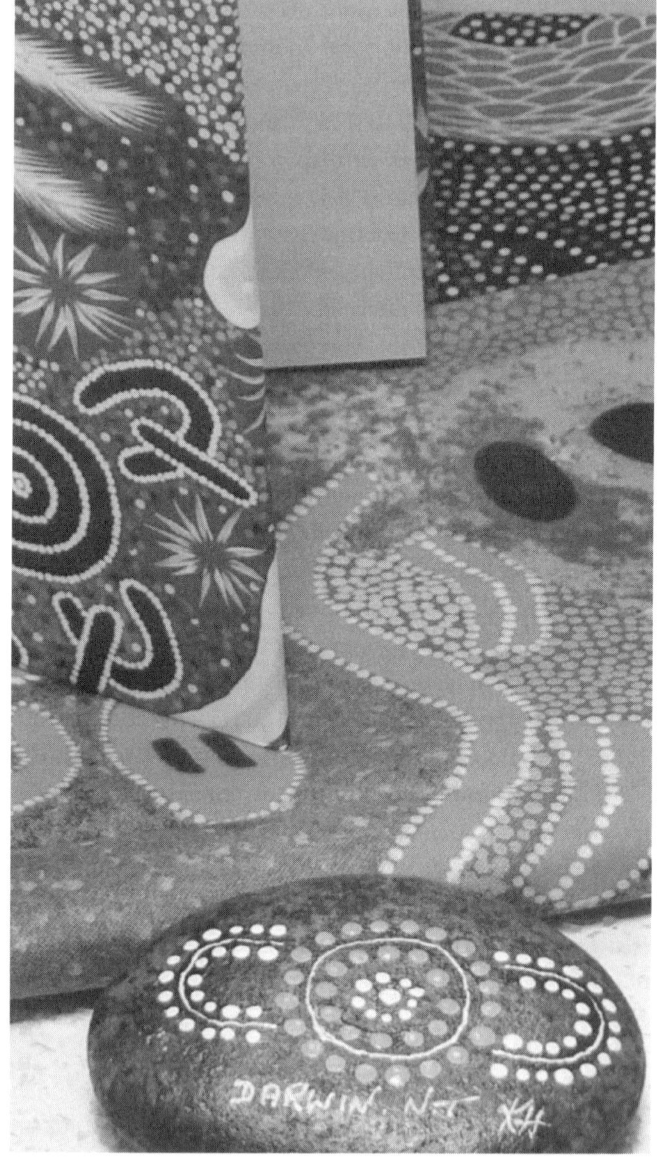
DARWIN, N.T

in the desert area), allowed Papunya Tula a fifteen years' start on the others to win market share (National Gallery of Victoria 2006).

This strange crossover of sacred law, political necessity, and marketing opportunity continues in the art center movement today.

In a report undertaken by Desart, the association of Aboriginal art centers, the lack of interest within many art centers in developing markets, meeting existing demand and quality control, and generally treating the art as product, are put down to the difficult social setting in which they work. It seems not to be a value for the stakeholders who the report addresses that the art center would be run solely for the cultural expression of the communities.

This is because the government money has been granted to art centers as part of policies for economic development. Australian governments have not historically funded cultural resilience. There are also many signs in the Australian setting that governments do not fund Aboriginal strength, but only weakness. *Your culture can survive as long as it will fit on a teatowel.*

Yet treating art centers as businesses cuts close to the bone, as does expecting Western business practice in the outback in the wake of dispossession and conquer. It is not that the Australian taxpayer does not "have a right" to see funds acquitted properly—it is just that the taxpayer has not taken the board out of its own eye. The enormity of the debt in the other ledger, the one that would calculate the value of traditional ownership of the land, just makes such petty bookkeeping grotesque.

The "community" in community art centers also sets up the dissonance with European practice; the "art" is a collective property, much more like what the European regards as "science," yet the marketability of it creates the irony that in some desert communities the best source of employment is to become an artist.

What happens when Tommy Watson becomes so famous that the art center needs him, more than he needs it, to be an artist? Given that Central Desert art, although it "deserves to be regarded as a movement"

(*Landmarks*), lapses into a political cause just as readily, then Tommy Watson becomes obligated in a way Mark Rothko was not, to the community that bred him. His celebrity and his social responsibilities flow from his Aboriginality, differently from Rothko's émigré past, because painting the *jukurrpa* was first and foremost a collective strategy for cultural survival and spiritual integrity, in country turned hostile.

In *Bad Aboriginal Art*, Eric Michaels remarks on the absence of criteria for judging Aboriginal art that would make it possible to build a credible place as "fine art" for the work, in art history or in the art market (Michaels 1994). Since the essay was written in 1988, there has been a development in the critical appreciation of work at the "gallery" end of the market. (See, for example, Bardon 2004; Nicholls and North 2001; Myers 2002).

What are the emerging criteria for judging of this genre? Can one say, for example, of "carpetbagging" canvases produced in bulk in the Motel Nancy in Alice Springs, or on private properties around the area, that they are not "good" paintings? A lack of luster can be seen in some of this work, a repetitive cursory feel, and laziness of technique. In galleries throughout Australia's cities there are canvases authenticated as Petyarre or Kngwarreye that are far from the luminescence of their museum-quality canvases. But can one yet enumerate the qualities that make this judgment more than just a matter of personal taste?

Michaels does not attempt this aesthetic or art historical task; he raises a few challenges for it, however, that are instructive. A critical perspective that gave this art its due would need to be able to meet these challenges, in order to judge the art on its own terms.

The different place of the artist in Indigenous culture, and the valuing of the perpetuation of tradition, means that authorization, rather than authenticity, is the issue for Indigenous people. As Michaels puts it, plagiarism is not possible for the Warlpiri, and theft is the greatest threat.

This flies in the face, as he argues, of the entrenched European value of the signature which accords a canvas a place in a series based on the individual artist whose style it exhibits, thus interpolating it into the currency of the tradition and thereby of the market.

Because cultural knowledge is owned differently in Indigenous contexts, the "hand of the artist" is differently valued. It is usual, for example, in Indigenous art production for relatives to be involved in undertaking much of the work, such as the in-fill of dotting, making the owner of the Dreaming more akin to an art director than a painter in European parlance.

This analogy is not coincidental, since the design tradition of Indigenous Australia took place alongside ceremonial activities—what we might identify as the involvement of painting in theater, opera, or dance production. But of course this is counterposed to fine art—"museum art"—in the Western version of the art world. While Diaghilev is acclaimed as a genius, it is Picasso who is the currency of it.

Of course there are models in the Western art tradition of the collaborative style of production, too: from the studios of the old masters to Andy Warhol's factory, in the practice of artists such as Jeff Koons and Patricia Piccinini, and the traditional collaboration of master printers with printmakers in etching and lithography (for example, in the work of Helen Frankenthaler).

The "myth" of cultural purity and the valuing of Aboriginal art primarily as "art of the other" (in the style of the Musée du quai Branly) seriously occludes its aesthetic qualities. These arise from its neologism, borne of the meeting of traditional designs and contemporary materials, of Aboriginal and European cultural production specifications.

But the central difficulty Michaels identifies for a critical practice emanates from the *"mise en discours"* through which Aboriginal paintings are positioned for sale in contemporary markets. The work is represented as *authentic* in its sacred tradition, and true to its "enabling" Dreaming story. This peculiarity confounds an aesthetic valuation of the work as fine art. The anchoring of the painting in its cultural context restricts its generalization as the Kantian universal prized as "art for art's sake."

These values may be clichéd, and may be even incoherent, but they still underwrite the prestige of fine art in Western culture.

Many paintings in the European tradition, too, require an understanding of mythology for their appreciation. And speaking of cliché, nothing could be more romantic than the story of genius in da Vinci or of suffering in Van Gogh. But it is an enabling fiction of modernism, at least, that the image can stand alone—and of postmodernism, that it *must*, like the text without a guarantee of an author.

To "stand alone" like this, an artwork must be carefully balanced on the cultural prejudices of the time. To be *Untitled*, as opposed to merely obscure, a canvas must be precisely positioned within its milieu. We can see the developing of this positioning in the twenty years since *Bad Aboriginal Art*.

The use of a narrative to legitimate an image marked the passage of the art from ceremony to canvas. At the beginning of Aboriginal art's crossing from the anthropological to the art historical, these stories were seen as necessary to establish the art as worthy of collection. Yet now, as the genre is becoming established in auction houses and public collections, nationally and internationally, we see admiration focusing on those paintings that no longer burden us with their reference but simply represent the enigmatic surface of a venerable culture.

The first paintings came from the need of the Aboriginal elders to convince the Europeans of their entitlement to their land, while persuading their own children to keep faith with the traditions. "The situation I worked in at Yuendumu demonstrated unequivocally that the Warlpiri painting I saw, even if it accepts the label 'traditional' as a marketing strategy, in fact arises out of conditions of historical struggle and expresses the contradictions of its production. This is really where its value and interest as 'serious' fine art lies; furthermore, it may also be the source of its social legitimacy" (Michaels 146).

The claim that the genre would be judged increasingly on "the contradictions of its production" seems borne out by subsequent events. The popularity of the work, as seen through the demand for group and solo exhibitions of the genre, emphasizes the contrasts between new materials and techniques ("Abstract Expressionism" ubiquitously cited) and "the oldest continuing tradition in the world."

The catalog for the 2006 exhibition "Dreaming Their Way" at the National Museum of Women in the Arts in Washington, D.C. puts the contradiction this way: "Most public museums have struggled to understand how contemporary Aboriginal art fits in to the story of world art. For museums with an emphasis on social and cultural history, Indigenous Australian art can be considered to be aesthetically based and market focused. Conversely, art museums often categorize the work as ethnographic and anthropological" (Price and Nicholson 2006:16).

It flies in the face of traditional contexts, but for the purposes of contemporary Indigenous acrylic art, display and dissemination are the point. Sale of the canvases is the desired end, publishing the image as a claim to title over land. Economic survival, title to land—these are the dominating conditions of Aboriginal Australia.

The image is no less a property claim in Indigenous as in European law. But today, while customary law may be acknowledged, it is not observed. Anyone anywhere can "own" a Dreaming image, although they may never seek or be given the knowledge it represents. Indeed, it may not be representable as proposition at all. The designs prompt a marking of awareness, by bringing to awareness a bodily familiarity with desert experiences through a shorthand of signs. The Dreaming stories, in their appearing partly as mnemonics for carrying cultural formations, are fetishized when constructed as "narrative" by the anthropologist or critic.

Fred Myers contributes to an understanding of how the movement came to be so successful, by describing the different "producers" of meaning in the art—the painters, the art advisers, the purchasers. This approach works, because the meanings are and have been quite different for the different groups, and yet in a kind of relay action have stimulated the "making of an Aboriginal high art" (Myers 2002).

Myers's stories about being in the field are more interesting, and telling, than his attempts to think the place of ethnography in postmodern global culture. Perhaps his proselytizing is provoked by Eric Michaels's attack on him in "'If all anthropologists are liars…'" (Michaels 1994). The critique Michaels offered there, of Myers's earlier work on the Pintupi, was that, for all his focus on the forming of subjectivity and the meaning of events in the subjective lives of his subjects, Myers does not find a way to reflect on his own subject formation in this process. And, as such, although it has a postcolonial veneer, Michaels finds his work still prey to the problems that beset anthropology as a privileged "view from nowhere."

This disturbing question about the subjectivity of the "white Aboriginal studies scholar" is more than evident, and ongoing, across the field, not only in scholarly papers on culture offered by anthropologists. Testimony is offered beyond academic audiences to the land councils and courts, establishing real-time economic benefits to the Indigenous. Anthropology has been the great white gatekeeper in Australian Indigenous politics, whose role has been intensified as the missions faded and the legal-bureaucratic apparatus developed to apportion indigeneity.

The traditional Aboriginal groups maintaining active cultural links to country, almost by virtue of this link, do not speak, let alone write, English well enough to negotiate this apparatus alone. Anthropologists speak for them, and make a considerable personal investment in these groups to do so.

Myers, for example, attests to this when he reveals the day-to-day snippets from his "fieldwork" living with the Pintupi people. By his own admission, the recording of the Dreaming stories behind the paintings was a job he took up in order to "make himself useful." In effect, it gave him a position in the group from where he could receive cultural knowledge.

The "interpreter" of paintings that apparently required interpretation for sale, would have a strong entry point into cultural matters that were otherwise closed to outsiders. Myers is able to relate the way circumstantial matters affected the way he did this job of "translating" and the slips and errors along the way.

A persisting subtext in Myers's narrations is the tendentiousness of the Aboriginal engagement with him about this knowledge. The Pintupi know it means something, to him and to them. They are aware that he needs exclusive knowledge to be thought an expert on them, and they need "their" expert to narrate their stories of entitlement. Myers's idea of a fine-grained account of the different producers of meaning in the field of Aboriginal cultural observation is a promising perspective, especially including scrutiny of the most authoritative of those producers, the ethnographer.

Examples of cultural research with explicit subject projections for the ethnographer include Eric Michaels on observing the beginnings of Warlpiri painting on the *Yuendumu Doors* (1987) and Jennifer Deger's involvement in the media projects of Yolngu in *Shimmering Screens* (2006).

But one aspect of the art that Michaels's assessment of its fine art potential does not take into account is its "pictorial logic," a consistency within the projection of the images themselves that solicit admiration for the rendering of something as *painterly*. The emerging "giants" of the genre have captivated this painting space through techniques that belong to the visual alone, whatever their reference and "back-story." In art criticism of Clifford Possum Tjapaltjarri, for example, or Emily Kngwarreye, this work is finding its way into capitalized Art on the strength of its visual and haptic projections.

This may have been inevitable, given the difficulty of interpreting this work from an informed cultural perspective; very few art critics are also versed in Aboriginal lore. But the effects of the paintings themselves, their creating of exciting "pictorial facts" (Deleuze 2003:160), allows this genre to slip the noose of the anthropological and ethnographic and produce new terms for its judgment.

Culture

How are people from widely differing cultural perspectives able to come together in any sense of the "global"? It is not through rational argument that these encounters more often take place. We live in eras that, however distinct from each other—the Central Desert, Melbourne and Sydney, New York and London, or the Sudan—are colonized by the image.

The image circulates—from the high art canvas to the mass media televised news bulletin—throughout the "Real World," soliciting viewers to respond as they can. And these responses are constituted from the feelings called up in viewers through the action of the image. From sympathy to envy, from anger to shame, affects are mobilized that can "make love or war"—build community and identity, or destroy unity and ignite paranoia.

Global Art, Local Knowledge

The extraordinary story of Aboriginal acrylic art, simultaneously a contemporary style event and a reinvention of a long-standing sacred art, is made more poignant by the troubled nature of life in the outback communities, revealed recently in various government interventions.

While the economic success of the art holds out an almost utopic prospect of Indigenous cultural renaissance, it is poverty, violence, and third-world living standards in these remote communities that remain the present reality (cf. Skelton 2010). Can Aboriginal art help make indigenous ways of life viable, as it has promised? Or will it just make investors and art dealers rich?

In 2007, France opened the new Musée du quai Branly, featuring the art of Australian Aborigines not only in its collection but incorporated as contemporary elements in its internationally lauded Enzo Piano design building. And at a Sotheby's auction in Melbourne in the same year, a canvas by an Aboriginal artist fetched a record $2.4 million. The AAMU museum for contemporary Aboriginal art has become established in Utrecht as a permanent display of Aboriginal art, and several other museums have hosted exhibitions (for example, "Remembering Forward" at the Museum Ludwig in Cologne in 2010).

The art is moving toward an extraordinary location in fine art—some are calling it the last great new art movement of the twentieth century. Prices at auction for museum-quality paintings suggest that this art is moving out of the artifact niche and into full membership of contemporary art. Aboriginal culture is still mostly known through anthropologists' translation, and the art is still sold attached to stories that were thought essential to its appreciation. But increasingly it is possible to delight in this art purely for its visuality, for the joy of its color and the vivacity of its line.

Aboriginal artists are used to their designs serving economic ends. Traditionally embedded in ritual and ceremonies, those designs signify to others in the Aboriginal world rights over country and resources. But contemporary Aboriginal art is also forming inside the Western global art scene, and is as much a product of it as it is of the Dreaming. This can lead to anxieties in the marketplace, where a certain desire for "authenticity" still imagines a traditional art and resists the view of it as contemporary, insisting that the artists know nothing of the wider art tradition and paint from their own culture.

But, at least in the case of major painters in this style, this seems unrealistic and a hindrance to critical appreciation. Serious attention to the aesthetic depth of these works develops as they move further from the range of "artifact" into the realm of contemporary art. But the context of the Musée shows that appreciation of the art is still stuck somewhere between anthropology and art history. The conceptual dilemma has economic effects—private galleries struggle at present to get the work accepted in major European art fairs, the places where sales and reputations are built.

The Australian example demonstrates the "Real World" case for better funding of activities like indigenous art centers that signal "cultural resilience." It shows that the social challenges in the communities and the success of the art *come from the same source.*

They come from the critical role that culture has in making people whole. *All of us* derive our values and sense of ourselves from our culture, and from the bonds, relations, and obligations that come with it. If this is torn apart over a prolonged period of time, any group will struggle to keep hold of the values that show them how to treat each other.

Two official reports, on the art industry and on child abuse in communities, came down within weeks of each other in 2007, and demonstrate the point. Amid claims that UK backpackers were painting didgeridoos sold as Aboriginal art, a Senate inquiry into Aboriginal art found that "carpetbagging," a highly damaging and disrespectful practice that preys on the fracture of community, threatened the reputation of the $250 million export industry. Unscrupulous dealers pay board and "expenses" to artists in return for the labor of painting canvases instead of paying the market rate for the paintings themselves. Artists often experience extreme pressure from younger relatives to work this way to earn money for the clan. But it results in the market being crowded with

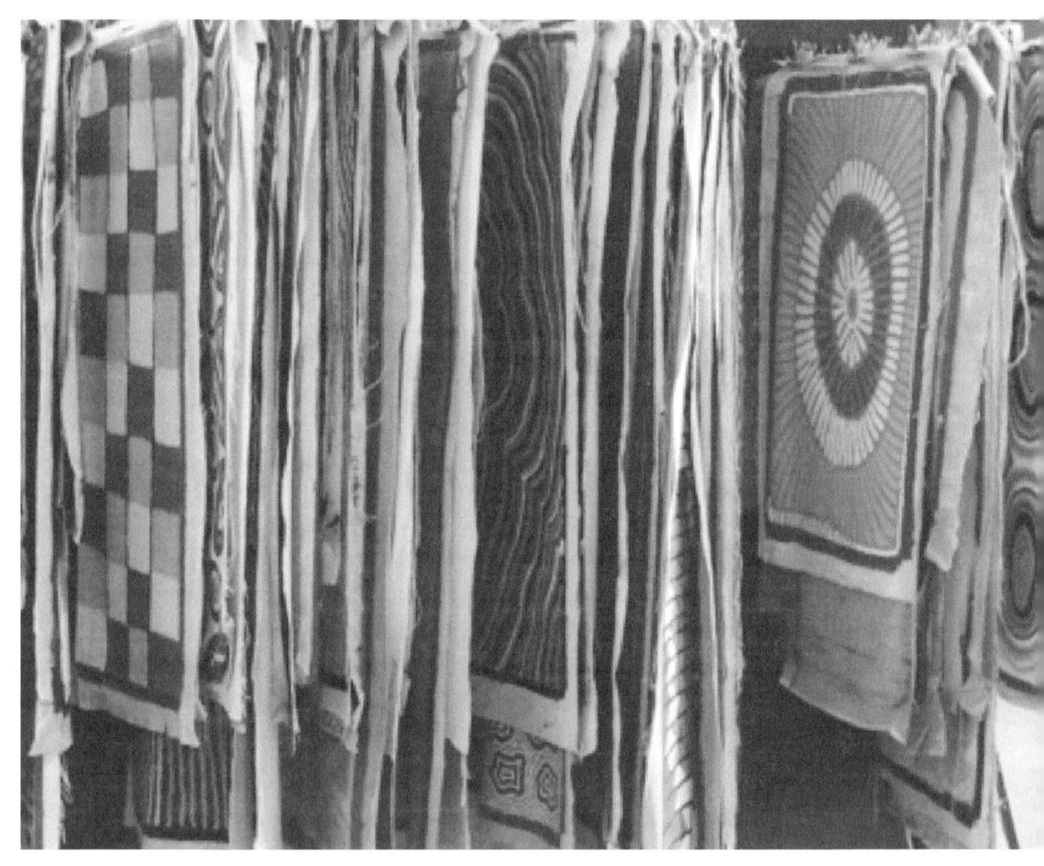

lesser quality work at prices undercutting the community art centers that have worked to build the reputations the carpetbagging cashes in on.

Simultaneously, the "Little Children Are Sacred" government report found child sexual abuse to be rife in Aboriginal communities "largely because of the breakdown of Aboriginal culture and society." The intervention in Indigenous communities that resulted from this report has been frankly on the model of assimilation. It aims to uphold Australian criminal law, not customary law, and to install white community standards of appropriate sexual activity and child rearing. And the move to abolish or suspend land permits, some fear, would continue the disbanding of traditional Aboriginal connection to country that has characterized much of the last century.

It seems everyone has a view. For or against, it is part of the culture—and our political education—that "everyone is entitled to their opinion." Ordinary Australians do not hesitate to make a judgment on Indigenous communities, even though most have not been there and rarely meet an Indigenous person.

But the self-certainty of Western perspectives can become unsettled when you start to explore Aboriginal country and its art. Ironically, you start to see what ethnographers have called the "European eye," the gaze that commonly goes uninterrupted and unanalyzed in regarding the cultures of others.

Despite the rough-and-ready look of outback places, there is a freedom and expansiveness there that many might envy. After all, the state of ordinary Western values can sometimes seem spiritually pauce. And struggling with substances that numb the void is not the preserve of Aboriginal Australia.

Wider Australia seems to expect Aboriginal people to give up on their culture and "move into town." A government committee recommended in 2007 that the aim should be for Indigenous Australians to become "employed in the private sector"—a de facto demand to resettle where there is Western-style work for wages—by 2010. Across the postcolonial world, those in the West have not acknowledged what we are asking when we require others to live like us. Taking away other people's ways of life is not only a human rights issue; it is a breach of democracy. It indicts a nation that it would ask some of its citizens to sacrifice this much of themselves.

The many languages, cosmologies, and ways of living of Aboriginal people provide an extraordinary cultural opportunity. But there is no model in the Western world for economic and cultural renewal through sacred art, so perhaps it is unsurprising that this possibility for Aboriginal Australia is regarded with skepticism and even scorn. Artists are not valued highly elsewhere in Australia, if financial support is any measure—this even creates some resentment toward the success of Indigenous art in other art circles. Spiritual satisfaction and aesthetic value are primarily seen as a private concern, as an individual responsibility—and sometimes, perhaps, as a luxury that ordinary Australia cannot afford.

It is unlikely that government policy will come to terms with an Aboriginal worldview, in which art and culture are communal property for which everyone is responsible for laboring and in which all share the return. It would take a remarkable sea change for policy priorities to shift eyes from the prize of mineral wealth locked up in Aboriginal lands. It would take an *epiphany* in Australian white culture to recognize the cultural variety as something that might enrich the nation as much as the resources boom has.

Marketable art is about reception, not production. Whatever the art means to its painters—and it is full of meaning to Indigenous people—for investors and gallery-goers Aboriginal art has two standout features to give it value: it is beautiful and it is scarce. On these two criteria, the painting has a big future.

In the midst of the travesties and tragedy of remote communities, it is a small miracle that anything is left of Aboriginal culture at all. But if the art is that miracle, it is because of the healing that painting up country brings about. The success of the art shows that some Aboriginal people

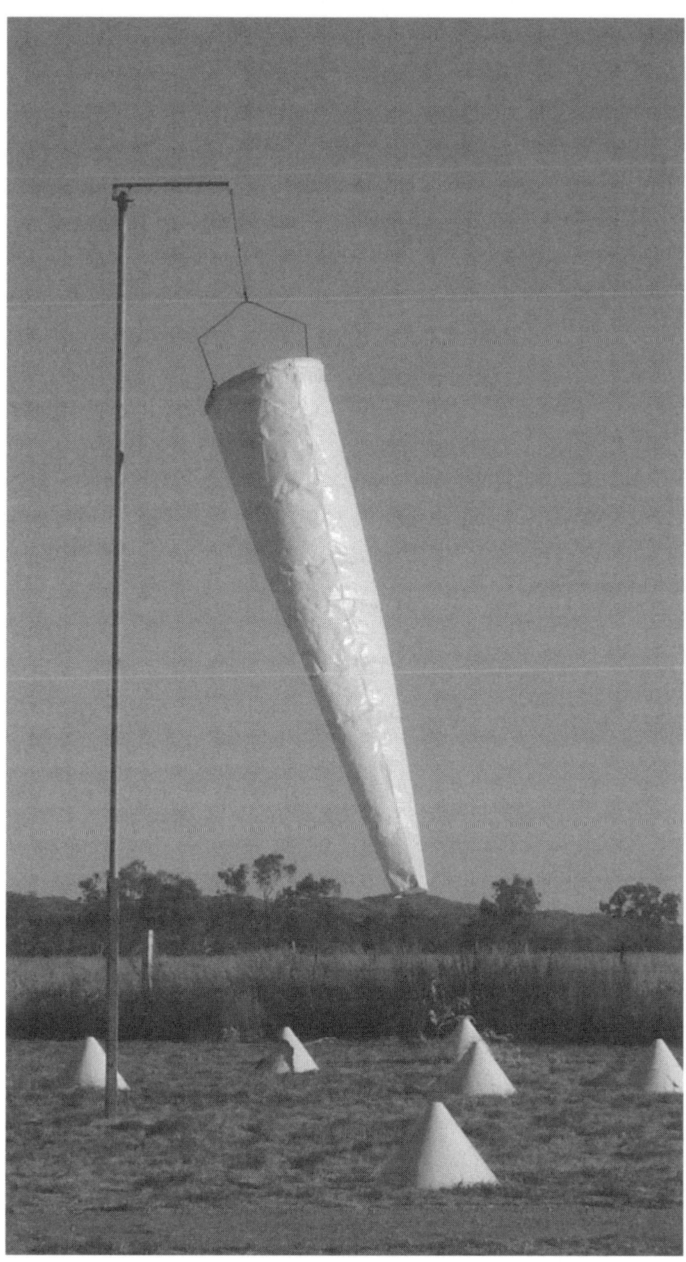

are rebuilding value by reviving their cultural life and, where required, reinventing it. This suggests it is genuinely sacred art—anthropologists such as Jennifer Biddle argue that the painting is a way of Aboriginal people *making* country, of creating the link with the world of Dreaming in the present, and not merely of showing it.

Seen from the air, the features of the desert country are differentiated only by color and contrasts in tone. There are few other features across the whole terrain around a circular horizon. The worn serrations of occasional mountain ranges, red and green, and the startling white and brown circles of salt lakes are laid out like huge Aboriginal acrylic paintings. By an inspiring alchemy of grief and fortitude, the outback has become the *art-back*, a place where suffering, tradition, and dispossession are coming back to us as the beauty and joy of color and line on canvas.

The Idea of the Museum

Despite its evident centrality to the modern experience of art, the museum is almost entirely absent as idea or institution from the contemporary literature of philosophical aesthetics. One needs to turn to cultural studies or ethnography to find an awareness of the collection as a force in cultural and aesthetic formation. (See, for example, Dibley 2007.)

For the museum, which is the ubiquitous medium of art experience, to fail to be discussed, to have no apparent significance for the philosophical discourse of the time, needs an explanation. It is due to a prevailing but old-fashioned commitment—one as old as Kant—to the work of art as being "for its own sake." This is to say, art not tied to function or desire but appreciated, as Kant would have it, with disinterested pleasure.

The slogan of "art for art's sake" presents the museum or gallery as the appropriate housing for art today, as opposed to the church or the palace in previous times. The museum or gallery is the habitat of art;

we know this because it seems to be completely natural for it to be displayed there, hanging on walls for the contemplative enjoyment of the spectator.

But the museum, despite its seeming naturalness, carries a message unlike the one carried by the church or the palace. The space of the museum is secular, receptive to the display (but not the fervor) of all kinds of faith. It is democratic too, since it can turn anything displayed in its space into an object for an aesthetic regard. These two assumptions mirror more generally the image of the modern nation-state, whose members are citizens, not believers or aristocrats.

The idea of the museum also gives us to believe that physical context is somehow *not* the point. To view Cézanne's work in the Musée d'Orsay or the Museum of Modern Art is to be offered the "same" aesthetic experience. Somehow art transcends—or at least is thought to move through and across—social and historical constraints, so that we can look at something even in the gallery devoted to Aboriginal art and expect it to communicate with us aesthetically.

This too is an assumption from a wider political sphere, in which differences between people are merely variegations in a pattern of basic equality. But this is quite an assumption to make about art. To imagine that a sacred object, for example, can be taken out of any temple in Southeast Asia or even out of a medieval European cathedral, let alone out of a ritual ceremony in a nomadic culture, and made to work as an aesthetic object in contemporary London, in a Victorian-style public building supported by the taxes of the populace, involves *several* complicated but invisible assumptions.

Among other things, it assumes that the object is the same in all times and places. But this assumption is challenged the moment we think of the obvious fact that, to the devotee in the temple, the object was sacred and carried in some sense proximity to the holy. Although this adds to its aesthetic charm when relocated in our time and place, it is clear that our appreciation does not spring from responding to this aspect of its existence. The assumption that this does not matter to the viewing of an object that it is originally viewed as sacred becomes an imperious assumption about the unimportance of its origin.

Likewise, the assumption that the art work is timeless ignores its curatorial realities. Paint is a material that changes across time. Art is constructed from materials, or anyway takes on material form, but some materials are more or less durable than others. This question of duration is related to the very question of art's material, its materiality, and yet the idea of art as transcending its context steps right over this.

Many now-famous artistic statements, like those of Marcel Duchamp, Yves Klein, and Andy Warhol, evoke the museum art's *shadow*—the commodity of the department store. These explore the relationship between the institution of high art and the institution of commodification. There are telltale parallels between Macy's and MOMA.

They are not unrelated physically, being large public spaces dedicated to display. But in counterpoint to the idea of being able to buy anything, available in the department store, the gallery presents the converse; you can buy nothing. The ethos states: this stuff is priceless. And yet we all know that there is a market in art; we all know that these paintings and other objects are bought and sold for a great deal of money.

This is not unrelated to a seemingly peripheral adjunct to the gallery space: the shop and the café. In fact, the presence of these two "comfort zones" in the realm of aesthetic contemplation is a reference to a whole mode of production for the art world, supported through the idea of commodification. You can buy in the museum shop representations of the art on the walls of its galleries; you can even buy the announcements of its displays as big posters, and you might be tempted to because they are colorful. To buy a print of an item in the collection because you like the image is a genuine souvenir, a way of recalling the art world once we move outside it.

The commodity character of art works is recognized and even celebrated with increasing frankness. The "blockbuster" exhibitions bring a particular version of art within the scope of mass spectators—a physical encounter with the work of art that one otherwise only sees in reproduction, i.e., *without* its material. But it also brings a particular interpretation of the history of art, and even of its philosophy, through the inclusions and excisions that curation has produced.

Perhaps, then, the museum space is not as secular as it seems, since it offers to "bless" particular moments of creation and to "transubstantiate" representations into points on the graph of art history. The public buildings that house museums can be reminiscent of churches and cathedrals and there is a kind of sacrilizing of art embodied in them.

If aesthetic experience is potentially universal, nevertheless, variations in the understanding and appreciation of art commonly do occur. They are put down to taste; that is, they are represented quite paradoxically as a matter of individual ability, or the individual eye. The process of democratizing what was a set of aristocratic values in the appreciation of art and the cultivation of taste is consistent with the European social history of being enlightened. It emerges from the modern revolutions, and it is not just art that is involved—philosophy, social organization, and political economy all moved with it. But art is an interesting example, since art can somehow go around our heads and into our sentiments to produce a more naturalized kind of experience. "I don't know much about art, but I know what I like."

The irony is that while the museum represents art as if it were for its own sake—that is, without any other function but to be art—this turns out to be its function. Reifying art from its social context in this way, withdrawing it from a history and social function, is part of the purpose of art. Art is a social function like any other; it enlists you in its values or it excludes you, it rewards you, or it makes you feel outside it, and it reinforces many series of complicated hierarchies.

The museum has also been described as a repository where the history of art is made visible. But perhaps we could go further and say it is where the history of art is made. For example, the setting up of a gallery for Aboriginal art was a late addition to the Art Gallery of New South Wales, in Sydney, which is why it is in a new wing. The Aboriginal artifact was not in the purview of art when the gallery was originally established in 1874. The growing edge of art history is literally represented in the blocks on the floor plan.

Clifford talks about the transformation of objects from artifacts to art in "On Collecting Art and Culture" (Clifford 1998). He depicts the movement of aesthetic meanings in a field divided by the polarities of art and culture and authentic and inauthentic. Since 1800, the domains of art and culture have become thought of as the domains of human value, he asserts, and in these domains are mirrored our own views of ourselves.

Clifford views collecting as a way of producing identity, personal and national, that in the Western mode is typically appropriative, that is, to do with making something "your own." As well as describing these domains and the history of traffic between them, Clifford also argues that *writing* about cultures and about art becomes a kind of collecting. He claims that ethnography, for example, is the collecting of knowledge so as to produce narratives about being Western and non-Western (in the case of Margaret Mead), or modern and primitive (Lévi-Strauss).

But Clifford suggests that today this cultural "self-assembling," through the means of the scientific or art collection, cannot be unselfconscious. The contemporary curator knows that what she presents as a historical (or other) ordering is her own narrative, and may even use this fact to enhance her curation.

It may be that curation is now possible that questions its own authority, and which highlights for the viewer the unstable and wish-fulfilling thoughts behind the well-accepted history of the objects from a particular time and a place.

More commonly, the museum moves toward the manipulations of marketing in its search for identity. The enjoining of the museum to "infotainment" and the making of national identity on the model of a service industry (Dibley 2007) brings it closer still to the department store.

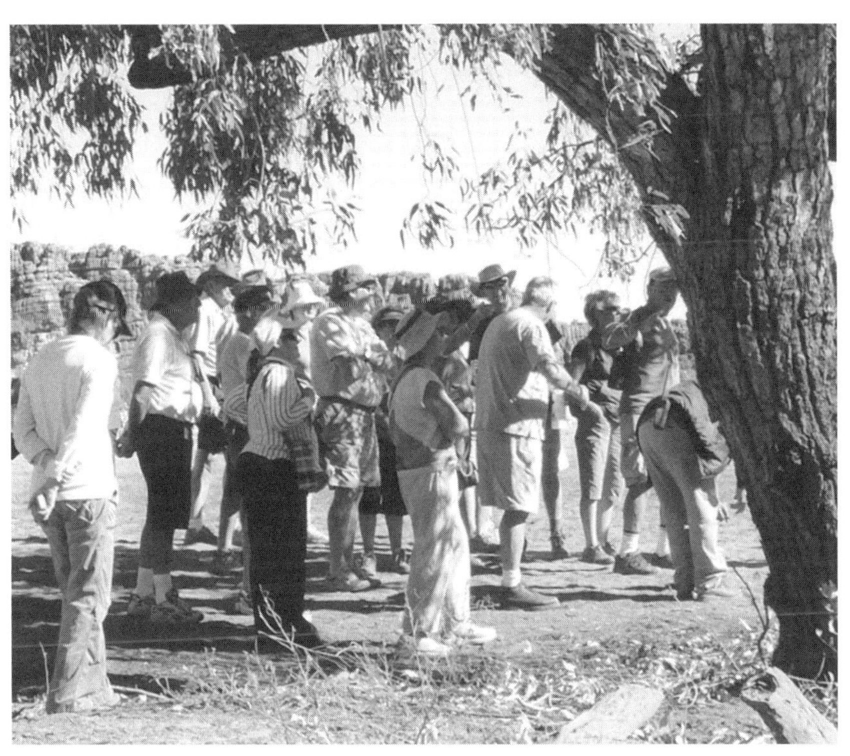

In Translation

The Musée du quai Branly in Paris is an opportunity missed. It others the others, the third world or the first nations, as they are more politely known (but do we have a definition for the first world, second world, and who is in each?) *Là où dialoguent les cultures,* its slogan reads. Perhaps this explains the remarkable muddle of the museum, its lack of cohesion? Located somewhere near where the postcolonial imagination fails, where the image falls into sentiment, cliché, or shock (Sontag 2003).

When I encounter a new image from another culture, I also approach it deeply immersed in my own cultural arrangements which are also material potentialities and impossibilities. The task of appreciating the new work is first a translation, but one which is open to the aesthetic dimension. By that I mean it is open through the material to an event of experience.

Walter Benjamin writes, in his celebrated paper on "The task of the translator": "The basic error of the translator is that he preserves the state in which his own language happens to be instead of allowing his language to be powerfully affected by the foreign tongue" (Benjamin 1996: 251).

The powerful affect evokes the aesthetic as an opening onto the domain of truth-making, which innovation could only happen if we relax our already organized understandings in favor of allowing something else to happen.

The metaphor of translation may be appropriate to cultural exchange, since language is very often the leading cultural artifact through which that exchange is initiated. Yet we cannot assume what, through translation, we come to understand. The possibility of translation—what it transmits, what it omits—might well be theorized as structurally aporetic. The notion of a communication of a vibration, as against that of information, captures the limit of the textual metaphor, which can occlude more material notions.

Being powerfully affected by the foreign tongue entails assuming that the material arrangements of language are integral to its ideas. But translation already assumes a more or less stable set of meanings in the languages that encounter each other. Even an open-ended notion of translation is limited in this way. Benjamin requests: "The translation must . . . form itself according to the manner of meaning of the original, to make both recognisable as the broken parts of a greater language, just as fragments are the broken part of a vessel" (Benjamin 1996: 251).

This postulates a greater language, a commonality of ideas and experience, that goes beyond the material expression of the individual language, and in which both can be compared. The image of fragments of a broken vessel becomes an even more poignant image of a fractured but common humanity in which the translation of experiences is possible. This "greater language," the larger vessel, is proposed as available in translation, to make it viable.

But what is needed is an exploration of the likelihood of that greater language; the formations of those intelligibilities, in which the languages, before their translation, take shape. The textual metaphor is not completely equal to the task, when it functions only as a model of exchange. We may lose some communication of the aesthetic experience in the translation.

The appeal of the textual metaphor generally in recent philosophies, to describe the making of meaning, arises in the anguish of the postcolonial, in which intelligibility cannot be assumed but must be negotiated. The trope of language has extended to include not only a set of vocalizations which make up a natural language, but any arrangement of elements which taken together generate meaning—from written marks to habits of dress and rules of kinship.

The domain of the semiotic is thus much larger than the "ordinary language" concept of language, designating a theoretical association between the production of meaning in language and the production of meaning in the social and conceptual domain. This is not strictly "mere metaphor," but an association that grows out of a material process that underlies this production.

A study of intelligibility suggests that meaning is a product of power as much as of truth. Indeed, truth is its product rather than its referent. And power always acts on something material —a body, an arrangement of spaces, a deployment of time, etc.

The aesthetic precedes the semiotic, in the sense that the aesthetic describes the arrangement of elements that bring out intelligibility as a material event. The aesthetic is that domain in which a formation emerges from any inchoate or disordered material. Its elements provide a challenge (Heidegger calls it "strife"; Deleuze and Guattari visualize it as vector forces on emergent planes), a challenge that assures there will always be innumerable possible meanings from a given set of elements. At the same time, their friction, as a product of their different qualities, will guarantee the specificity of each particular set.

The aesthetic composes material elements according to their character, at the same time as that aesthetic is composed by its materials, forming out of their peculiar resistances. In each case, an artist's aesthetic is referred to a particular challenge of elements—material, pictorial, historical—which leaves its mark on the canvas. The possibility of new painting lies in these innumerable occasions for manufacture out of these elements.

This is not to say that this is what the artist saw, or meant, let alone struggled for. The deep irony of appreciation, as with translation, is that intelligibility is produced for another, out of an arrangement of materials. Who can say what composition of concept and color, guilt and avarice, ignite the canvases of the "Indigenous other" for the European eye? Who is to say, or gainsay, what elements an artist, with what unconscious or deliberative genius, will be able to force into play of the social material at her disposal, on the canvas that she then presents to the appreciative eye?

So, we need to ask: what is happening in translation to the *difference* between one language or culture and another? Especially, where one

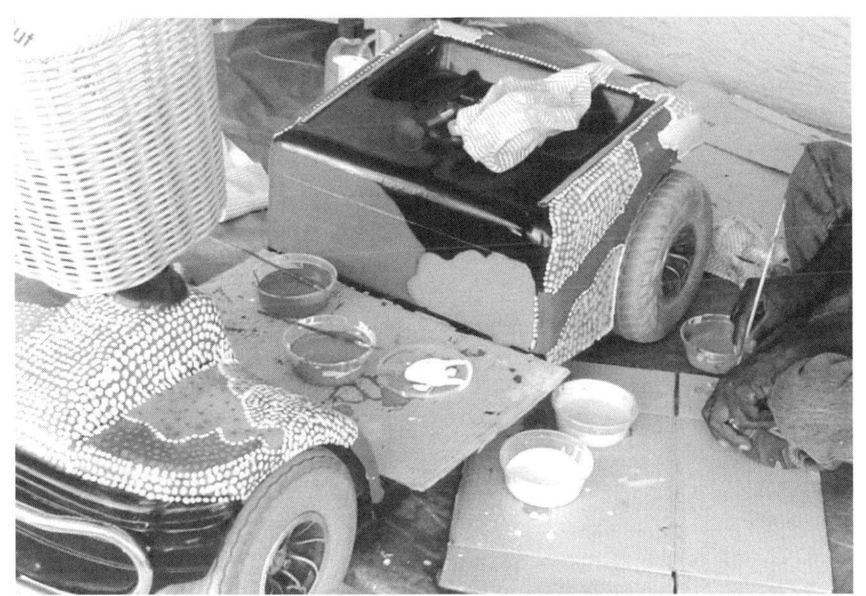

language dominates another, how faithful is the translation—and to *whom* is it faithful—to the culture it translates, or to the one it translates for?

A White Thing

The modern urban subject desires to save wilderness, respect other cultures, and know something about art, going to galleries, buying "fair trade," and voting green. The three belong together in a secular landscape, denuded of other forms of sacrament. Eco-tourism is whitefella worship.

"Aboriginal art is a white thing," runs Richard Bell's satirical slogan. Aboriginal art has been commodified "as a brand name product for the modern, tasteful market in white supremacy" (Grossman 2003:83), charges Marcia Langton. "It seems as if the artists themselves had walked into the nostalgic present from the mythic 'stone age.' Aeroplanes transported them to this nostalgic present in exhibition galleries in the art capitals of the Western world—New York, Paris and Berlin—and the artists carried mobile phones" (ibid.:82).

Langton is impatient with the market fetish for the authentic, observing pungently that Aboriginal art is "an artefact of the colonial encounter" (ibid.:86). The category of the indigenous is already completely contaminated by the colonial, by the notion of a culture that is indigenous to the place and simultaneously not in possession of it.

So, is Aboriginal art a White Thing? It is, because it is a fetishizing of another group's painting as essentially not white, as authentically different and arising from non-Western (nonscientific) beliefs.

It is not, inasmuch as it has provided one strong pathway to self-assertion for Aboriginal peoples that has gained them inter/national identity and recognition.

It is, since the designation of it as "Aboriginal" signals the whole knowledge-cluster of "culture," a category belonging to Western thought.

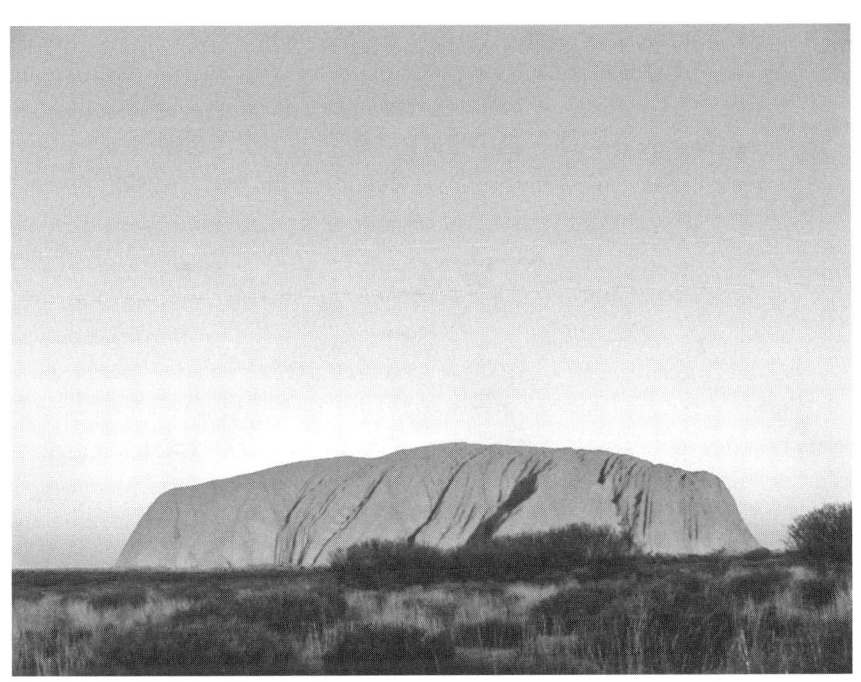

It is not, because what the artists are depicting refers to lore that is arcane and specific to groups of Aboriginal people, and known to white people only as observers. Even privileged observers such as anthropologists do not become Aboriginal by this lore being revealed to them. It belongs to a world in a real and exclusive sense, that is not the "white world."

It is, in that it was conceived as one white man's translation of Pintupi lore as art; it has worked and gained efficacy through the principles of Western art history and the Western art market, which its advisers, black and white, have strategically addressed.

It is not, since Aboriginal artists do not occupy positions in the Australian art establishment, receiving the financial rewards and peer recognition of this group. Instead, they are treated, at best, as distinguished visitors.

But, by the same token, maybe it is, in that all artists in Australia are somewhat despised, and art in general is bracketed with culture, religion, and other "soft options" that contrast with the deep reverence given to the "Real World" images of photographs and facts.

How could it be otherwise, when the image as the primary place of truth and the sacred is so intricately regulated in the Western globalizing world? The logic of the image underpins the intelligibility of "Aboriginal Art."

Image Logic

The format of ads for consumer technology is prescient. Think of the flyers that arrive in a suburban letterbox, spruiking everything from cosmetics to food, cameras to printers, and other means for the end of image representation.

These advertisements are schemas that lay out a kind of syntax for a "grammar of technology." The point is not so much what they specifically sell, but what they market generically—the way of thinking that has been described as "technological."

The association of ideas moves literally, vertically, horizontally. Via contiguity, the same sign ($), referring differently, serves to relate the series into the equivalence of commodity. Buy this—or this—or this. What can we observe about this way of thinking that might challenge us in our more traditional genres?

It presents an atemporal logic. "Best Brands, LATEST MODELS." The past has no purchase: if I include past terms, it is not to evoke causal consequences or to introduce a radical difference from the present. The Before-and-After shot operates through the mechanism of visual analogue.

It is a serial logic. Good—Better—Best. In whatever modes of differentiation the series is constructed—price, features, currency, brand name—it is grounded in similarity. The series connects terms, not through narrative, causal, or logical consequences, but through a more asequential logic, likeness (and predominantly visual likeness) that can be played on forward or rewind.

It determines a logic of the same. Equivalence produces legibility. Or (to adapt Derrida) iterability is the condition of its intelligibility. What produces the legibility of these terms is their similarity; it protects, supports, and promotes their differences into an intelligible discourse.

It signals a logic of the image. The image eats the word, in that there becomes no radical difference between their methods of signifying. Affect swallows meaning, in that there is no longer a profound distinction between signification and significance, and the link between sign and its referent dissolves.

This shift signifies a modulation in intelligibility. Narrative is overridden, argument eclipsed. Associative thinking prevails, in which there is a concern not with causes but with effects, an emphasis of surface over depth. In this overwhelming stream of image-logic, *the really different becomes radically invisible.*

Julia Kristeva gives us a metaphor for this: "Modern man is losing his soul, but he does not know it, for the psychic apparatus is what registers representations and their meaningful values for the subject. Unfortunately, that darkroom needs repair" (1995:8).

If we follow Kristeva's metaphor, the psychic apparatus is a darkroom, that is, a process by which sheets of light (and other sensory data) can be produced as meaningful marks. Just as the professional photographer knows how to influence the resulting image by varying a multitude of elements in the process (the aperture, the film speed, the developer, the enlarger), so the psyche produces meaning in images by subjecting it to the structures of desire. It is the engendering of *an affective connection through the production of a representation.*

If we stop there, content with the image as representing the real, then we accept this laminate of desire as fact. In effect, we prefer our fantasy over reality, a working definition of psychosis. Yet this presupposes that desire and reality can be prized apart.

The separation of reality from its image is a metaphysical gesture, one that—more precisely—separates the subject from its objects in the image. The image is a potent psychic technology for thinking of the world in terms of its technological potential, that is, as means to ends. By this I mean it is the image that can direct representation toward desire, express in the object *a desire accomplished,* in the most crude Freudian terms of wish fulfillment. Kristeva writes: "The rapture of the hallucination originates in the absence of boundaries between pleasure and reality, between truth and falsehood" (Kristeva 1995: 8).

But at the same time, and perhaps because of this, in Western philosophy the image is spared the rigor of the concept. The image is spared *for the affect* without which we *cannot* think, even though it is sacrificed to thought at a certain point in the logic of instrumental rationality. The image retains the color of this sacrifice, and remains the receptacle of it, of all that I am drawn to and connected with, despite my putative separation from my objects.

This explains perhaps why images, and aesthetic appreciation in general, are so sacred to the West, and why today they emerge as the obvious intellectually respectable way to spirituality. The modern bourgeois urban subject desires to "know something about art," going to galleries, collecting, etc. The epiphany would be the imageless image—the

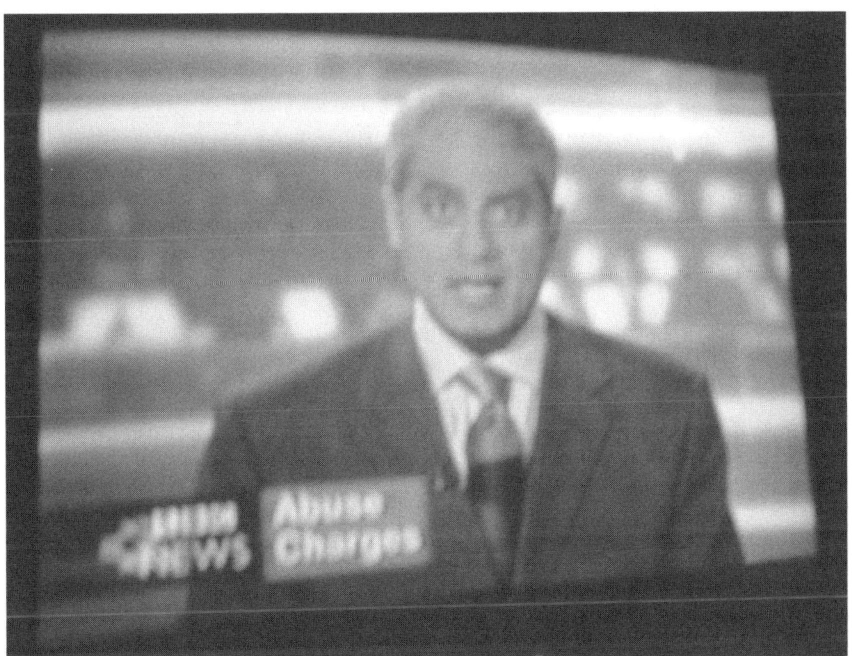
Abuse
Charges
NEWS

epitomous Rothko, for example—that asserts only a serial logic of sensation.

Kristeva writes in several places of the mystery of life and meaning that is joined in the sacred. In Kristeva's diagnosis, "the body conquers the invisible territory of the soul. . . . You are overwhelmed with images, they carry you away, they replace you, you are dreaming" (1995:8). This change in the psychical order could be momentous enough to be a new form of subjectivity, where the question shifts from "To be or not to be?" to "To take a pill or to talk?" Kristeva discerns the body, or at least a particular secularism in neuroscience and biology, to have called into question the *function* of the psychic apparatus: "If drugs do not take over your life, your wounds are 'healed' with images, and before you can speak about your states of the soul, you drown them in the world of mass media" (ibid.).

What do we get from the analysis of the darkroom of the soul? Is it a more sophisticated version of the so-called primitive anxiety that the photograph will capture your soul? Is the photograph, with its verisimilitude and its ubiquity taken together, capable of producing a new subjectivity?

Photojournalism

The privilege of the press photograph is to suggest a reality unmediated by representation. Naturally, this is a feint, for however realistic it appears, the photograph remains an image. As Barthes writes in "The Photographic Message":

> What is the content of the photographic message? What does the photograph transmit? By definition, the scene itself, the literal reality . . .
>
> In order to move from the reality to its photograph it is in no way necessary to divide up this reality into units and to constitute these units as signs. . . . Certainly the image is not the reality but at least it

is its perfect analogon and it is exactly this analogical perfection which, to common sense, defines the photograph. (ibid.:196)

The press photograph, "which is never an 'artistic' photograph," professes to be "a mechanical analogue of reality" (ibid.). Art photography nevertheless signals the realist paradox hidden in the press photograph. For example, in Indigenous photographer Tracey Moffatt's series *Scarred for Life*, the genre of photojournalism is itself borrowed for an artistic expression of the tragedy of the stolen generations, demonstrating it as a form of signification.

Barthes comments,

In front of a photograph, the feel of "denotation" or, if one prefers, of analogical plenitude, is so great that the description of a photograph is literally impossible; *to describe* consists precisely in joining to the denoted message a relay or second-order message derived from a code which is that of language and constituting in relation to the photographic analogue, however much care one takes to be exact, a connotation: to describe is thus not simply to be imprecise or incomplete, it is to change structures, to signify something different from what is shown. (1982:197–98)

The photographic paradox (a "structural and ethical paradox") then is this: "When one wants to be 'neutral,' 'objective,' one strives to copy reality meticulously, as though the analogical were a factor of resistance against the investment of values (such at least is the definition of aesthetic 'realism')" (ibid.:199).

Barthes goes on to consider the ways in which these appearances are deceptive; we can infer from our knowledge that the press photograph has been "chosen, composed, constructed and treated according to professional, aesthetic, or ideological norms"; likewise it is read, "connected more or less consciously by the public that consumes it to a traditional stock of signs" (ibid.:198).

The connotation carried by the photograph is "neither 'natural' nor 'artificial' but historical, 'cultural,'" suggests Barthes. "Its signs are gestures, attitudes, expressions, colors, or effects, endowed with certain meanings by virtue of the practice of a certain society: the link between signifier and signified remains, if not unmotivated, at least entirely historical" (ibid.:206).

Among other gestures, the photograph connotes "the perfection and plenitude of its analogy." The objectivity of the photograph is "mythical," in the structuralist sense—a signification of beliefs that give meaning to other cultural signs (ibid.:198).

Of course, photojournalism would be regarded in *common sense* as the antithesis of the sacred, but this only shows how deeply held the myth of the photograph as a record of the real is. The inherent religiosity invested in the famous image of the twin towers burning on September 11 makes the point. With its iconography of crucifixion, and the surrounding rhetoric of the axis of evil and the sanctity of American life, a reality sprung out of the image of apocalyptic change, and "the world will never be the same."

In more ways than many, this "media event" raises knowingness of the production of the real through images; for example, many have remarked on how this photo (and the video of the same events) are "like a disaster movie," its spectacular capture creating an iconic "photo-opportunity."

The myth of the separation of reality and image is paradoxically so strong that most viewers have no trouble identifying the press photograph as a *depiction of what happened*. We do so without awareness of its metaphysical origin, and invariably without skepticism as to its reference. It is as it purports to be. But aliveness to this mythical meaning structuring our view might come from considering the myths of others.

"These paintings make the claim that the landscape does speak and that it speaks directly to the initiated, and explains not only its own occurrence, but the order of the world" (Michaels 1987: 143). Despite the time he has spent in the desert with the painters, Michaels admits he has trouble accepting the claim of the paintings "in reality." The press photograph might prove his way into it, since it makes precisely the same claim: that reality speaks directly to the initiated in the image, explaining its own occurrence and the order of the world. In the photographs of 9/11, we see not only the burning skyscrapers which we accept as factual and not simulated, as they would be in a movie sequence: we also see that sequence coding the event as cataclysmic in the manner of that genre. We see sacrilege and historical forces at work, in the transmission of pixels to a screen, of dots to a page.

Such is the action also accorded to the icon in Byzantine art, which brings the devotee into direct communication with the sacred. This is dismissed today as superstition. Like other examples of instrumental thought, the belief in the reference of the photograph betrays its own religiosity not only as a record of the real, but also as *the only possible one.*

The representations of photojournalism are generically ubiquitous and forceful. This genre is often marked by trauma and violence, and it falls into the realm of the aesthetic while critically involved in commodification. Photojournalists use their images to arrest the attention of a knowing viewer bombarded with a constant stream of images, all soliciting affects of some sort. Such is life in the media. But the distinction between the representation and its historical event can slip from a reliable grasp, as atrocity and the tendentiousness of its image become more firmly glued together.

War correspondents have traded on the trauma of the battle in order to achieve their effect of bringing events from elsewhere to the attention of the reading/viewing public. Sometimes this enterprise is undertaken explicitly to bring to recognition the injustice being done in a part of the world we do not witness. Kevin Carter's photograph of the child and the vulture from Sudan is a case in point. It contains an importantly ambivalent relation to horror and trauma, since it depicts nothing in the present, except the menace of the near future. It is what we bring from our own knowledge of the world, what will happen next, that sickens us in this terrifying image. It won Carter the 1994 Pulitzer Prize.

This photograph operates to cultivate the loss of something previously unmissed: the Sudanese other, in the aftermath of European colonialism in Africa. Like the holocaust of World War II, this is an event that exceeds representation for Western subjects, who nevertheless must come to mourn it if there is to be justice.

The strength of the photograph's success in creating an affect for a representation of an event might be measured in the prestige of the Pulitzer, but also in Carter's own anguished suicide following the award of the prize. It is clear this photograph became potentially a type of *experience* for viewers. This photograph makes graphic the place of affects, and thereby of the body, in the production of "information."

Among the accolades for Carter came criticism for the culture of the photojournalist, for whom representation became more of an imperative than reality: "The man adjusting his lens to take just the right frame of her suffering might just as well be a predator, another vulture on the scene," as the *St. Petersburg* (Florida) *Times* is reputed to have commented. The ethical dilemma arises from an essential connotative property of the photograph that is strangely obscured—the photographer, as physically on the scene. The claim to reference and thereby to reality is underwritten by a body of human capacities and sensibilities who witnesses the event.

Yet, that body is *not quite* on the scene; certainly not in the same way that the little girl is on the scene. The photographer's equivocation, perhaps his judgment, that he could do more for the situation by photographing the scene than by saving the child, is unforgivable not only because of its seeming lack of humanity but for what it questions about photographic verisimilitude.

By invoking the photographer, the image puts into question its own "brute reality." This causes a disturbance in the epistemological frame that establishes the authority of the photograph. That frame grounds the superstition behind the press photograph as an objective record.

In Carter's photograph, the access to the real is too direct for comfort. For a photographer to be implied this way at the point of capture, a human subject with ethical choices beyond recording, makes all viewers of the scene somehow complicit in the travesty it represents. It raises the question, unbidden, *why a photograph there at that moment?* The mask slips briefly from the display of a reality that happens without construction or intervention. The belief in the scene, that it "really happened," *undermines* belief in its photographic objectivity.

And yet, this happens at the same time that the sacred function of the press photograph is demonstrated as a "natural" consequence of its reality—we believe what we see. This is a genuinely iconoclastic moment.

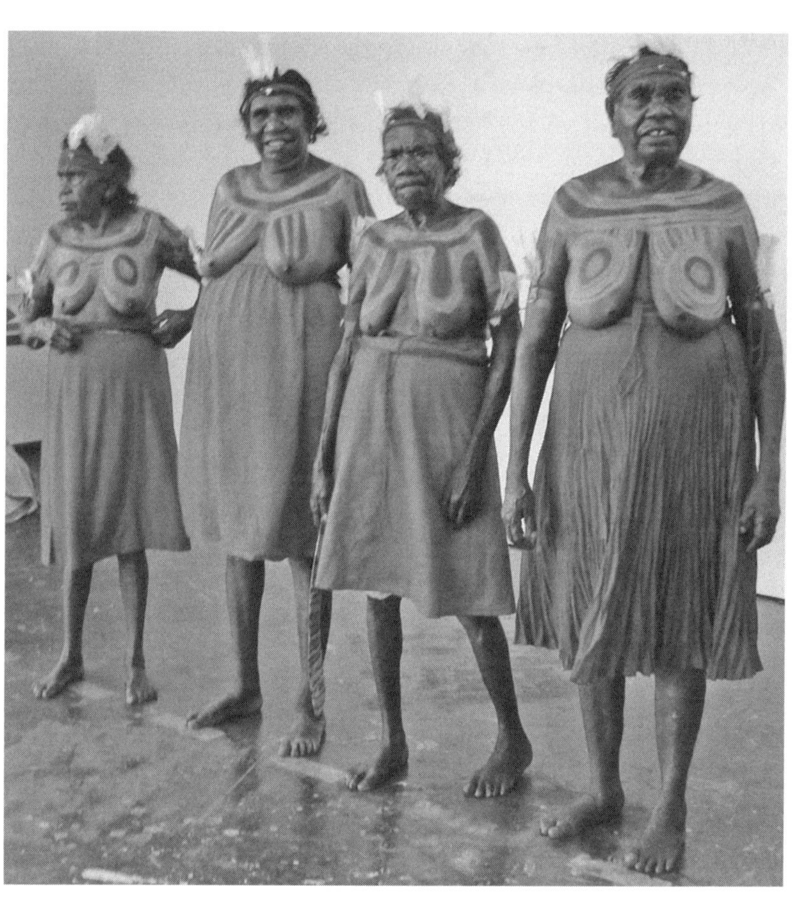

Gender

The point of desert women's painting, Biddle argues, is to "make a mark," a physical pressure or imprint on canvas in the same way that the *kurruwarri* were traditionally made on skin. In doing so, they evoke the imprint on country of the ancestors' actions; the fires, the dancing, the food, the fighting. The marks of these paintings are designed to produce the experience of being in that ceremony in that country, keeping the continuity of the Dreaming acting in the present.

And this matters now, more than ever, with the exile of traditional owners, their care confined to canvas where before they would have been "looking after country" in the flesh. In Dorothy Napangardi's delicate filaments of dots, Biddle finds Warlpiri culture as *torn* fabric, still potent although in fragments.

For the women, Biddle tells us, there is a specifically "breasted" way in which to view their attachment to country; the ceremonies that the *kurruwarri* reference are dances in which breasts are painted up and move in a rhythm conjuring the attachment of all to the land, like a suckled child attached to the mother.

This is a very different view of culture and place from the Western model of land ownership, but through the painting, there can be a magical extension of the Aboriginal world. Proximity to country is evoked for the viewer, even for the uninformed, by the vivacity of the surface itself, Biddle argues, and the spectator can enter country not so much by viewing as by *touching with the eye* its rhythm, color, texture, and contour.

The sacred nature of these canvases is embedded in the experience of viewing them. This is why Emily Kame Kngwarreye, when pressed by Christopher Hodges to describe what a canvas depicts, replies: *"You know."* The Dreaming is communicated directly in the feeling for the work (Neale 1998:33).

Stolen Culture

In 2007, the Australian federal government declared there was a "crisis" of child sexual and other abuse in these remote communities and sent in police and doctors over the heads of the autonomous Indigenous councils. The action followed from a disturbing government report released in the weeks before, titled "Little Children Are Sacred," citing alcohol and social breakdown as major causes of the routine neglect and abuse of Aboriginal children.

The Northern Territory Board of Inquiry reported that sexual abuse of Aboriginal children "is serious, widespread and often unreported." It goes unreported because frequently it is the child, and not the perpetrator, who is removed. Fears of the "stolen generation" era, when part-Aboriginal children were taken from Aboriginal mothers and brought up in foster homes and institutions, prevent present-day families from inviting scrutiny. As the report concludes, "Much of the violence and sexual abuse occurring in Territory communities is a reflection of past, current and continuing social problems which have developed over many decades."

The then federal government in response formed a "national emergency committee," passed legislation which explicitly overrode antidiscrimination laws, and allocated significant funds for medical and housing interventions on the condition that welfare payments were quarantined and some land permits suspended.

"Self-determination" implies that a group is of one mind. But few communities enfranchise their children, and the interests of children and those of the adults who have charge of them do not always coincide. Violence and sexual abuse against women and children speak to fracturing within groups, in which the stronger attack the weaker without compunction.

Self-determination can be hard in such a divided house. This is the experience of family law in the wider Australian community; witness the general failure to come to terms with levels of domestic violence and child abuse.

Aboriginal groups are fractured, since different members in them suffer differently in the postcolonial world, and each has lost different things. It seems plausible that the men are acutely dispossessed of prestige and authority, while women have retained more of their role, as carers for children, and may in fact have a heavier responsibility now, to manage family relations in the time of the breakdown of custom.

"There is no cultural defense to rape," the then treasurer Peter Costello said in federal parliament eailier that year. But some Indigenous women saw the assertion of *gender* politics, on the right or on the left, as contaminated by racism. They resented the assumption that white politicians (or feminists, for that matter) could speak on behalf of Indigenous women about their relations with Indigenous men, however problematic they may appear.

And—perhaps more to the point—they suspect the impulse that makes this violence, too, the fault of Indigenous people, along with their unemployment, poor health, and living conditions. Picking on Indigenous men for the violence blames the victim yet again and lets the white community off the hook yet again.

While the report of child abuse provided the cue to declare that self-determination is not working, it is arguably the history of assimilation that went *before* that set up much of the dysfunction with which the communities now struggle.

The "stolen generation" dismembered families, and the "sit down" money (welfare paid to Aboriginal people who came in to live on reserves

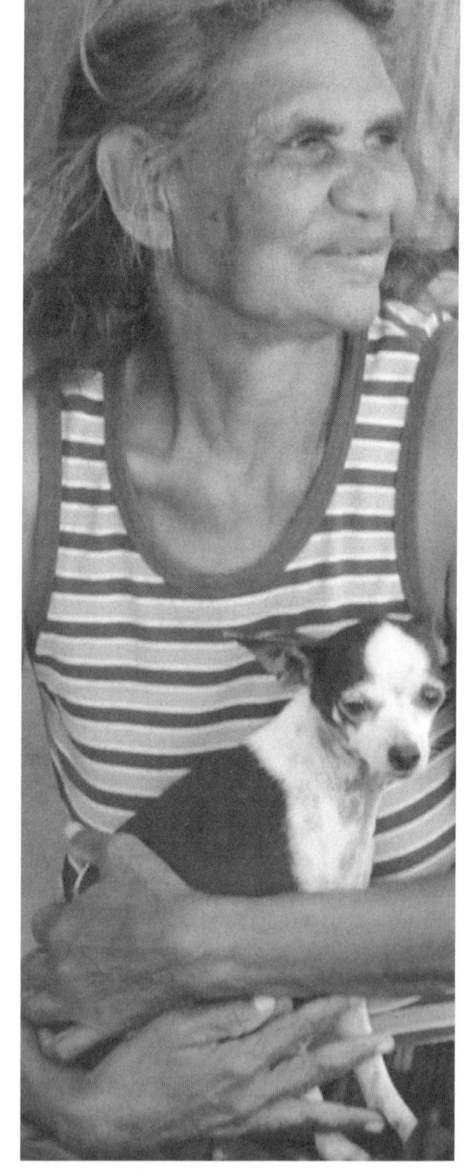

rather than on their traditional lands) paid by governments discouraged Aboriginal people from "taking care of country"; these ripped the guts out of the traditional ways of life. These groups were not given much in exchange except grief, poverty, and alcohol. Alcohol is the slow-release poison still acting in these communities as an effect of white settlement, as the report on child sexual abuse attests.

Better housing, education, and health support, especially for addiction, are obviously needed if these communities are to do better. All of which raises the question of why the gap, on these indicators, between indigenous and nonindigenous Australians has grown in the first place, and why it continues to shock. If government intervention could have worked, it would have, in the years of assimilation. And if autonomy were viable, it would have picked up where that administration left off in the 1970s.

Yet whitefella welfare, no less than the "liberal consensus" (Sutton 2009) has instead left the yawning gap between worlds, starting from life expectancy which, in 2010, was still ten years less for Indigenous people than for the wider Australian population.

It is not necessarily that Aboriginal approaches hold more hope for their people, given that they must take effect in a world compromised thoroughly by Western values. But it is unfortunately the converse: that Western philosophies alone cannot transform the questions of conflict into reconciliation, especially so since it is this obliteration of other philosophies, including Aboriginal, that has been "the other side" of the colonial coin in its genocidal ubiquity.

Little Children Are Sacred

The sacred, as announced by Kristeva in her epistolary exchange with Catherine Clément, *The Feminine and the Sacred*, is variously "life bearing meaning" (2001:14); "the mystery of the emergence of meaning (and its celebration)" (ibid.:13); "the impossible and nevertheless sustained connection between life and meaning" (ibid.:14).

Kristeva distinguishes this mystery from the technocratic "life without questions," the totalitarianism that seeks destruction of life, and the *zoos* that would leave life in the realm of the naturally instrumental.

Kristeva's concept of the "semiotic" and of the "chora," which she describes as "drives and their articulations," allows her to formulate the association of ideas theoretically: the semiotic is distinguished from the realm of signification with its propositions and judgements (1984:43).

The image here exceeds an art historical or aesthetic philosophical meaning. It is the image that reaches back *into the child*, where the word is first an aural image, and where that image is charged with affect as the part-object of the voice of its mother.

The association of ideas, according to Kristeva, is a corporeal process. This is not a body separate from its ideas, but a body that motivates its ideas, and that strings them together according to the movement of drive energy. By the time we are competent language-users this energy has become channeled in highly specific ways, and certain dispositions belong to certain orders of rationality.

Little Children Are Sacred.... The way in which the libidinal pleasures of the body transfer in Western life onto essential cultural operations like literacy, numeracy, and citizenship has been explored through the psychoanalysis of children, for example, in the work of Melanie Klein.

The maternal has a special place in the sacred, as generative of meaning and being. Its effects move outward in a double action, into real bodies and into the language used by those bodies. "Matrix" is a concept akin to that of genre, describing an element of signification that "participates without membership," which is also the way Derrida describes the law of genre.

In the Byzantine icon, the communion offered is with the Mother of God, that is, with the *image* of mother and child, the state preceding "the subject" in which we can discern its production. When Kristeva talks of life bearing meaning she conjures the extraordinary matrix between the body's energies and the psyche's images.

That matrix is set up in early childhood, with the first enunciations, the gestures, objects, and noises of little children. Because they are not yet sentences, generative grammar cannot find precise meaning in them, but they are the forerunners of words and sentences "in the sense that they separate an object from the subject, and attribute to it a semiotic fragment, which thereby becomes a signifier."

These fragments, while incoherent as language, bear meaning in the way they evince the intention to attribute something of something else.

"That this attribution is either metaphoric or metonymic ('woof-woof' says the dog, and all animals become 'woof-woof') is logically secondary to the fact that it constitutes…a positing of identity or difference, and that it represents the nucleus of judgment or proposition" (Kristeva 1984: 43).

This is a mystery, there's no doubt of it—the material of signs. The glamour of the icon lies in its remarkable evocation of the body becoming sign.

The connection is impossible and nevertheless sustained in every instance of symbolization, and in every iteration of affect that animates our representations. Little children are sacred because, in their dependence on their mothers, they carry this mystery for those of us who have long ago learned to live with it.

But the child is no "oceanic" baby; he is already alive to the mystery, squirming on his mother's lap and feeling her face for possibilities that will continue into adulthood as intellectual inquiry.

And since the image can deny contradiction *without being psychotic*, we cannot resist the image; it is a magnet for the eye. We want to commune with it and there discover our lost affects.

Other operations can intensify in the process of separation—mother from child, subject from object; violence, terror, consumption, and the experience of intense emotional states such as "dysphoria." Kristeva links these explicitly to the sociopolitical order that funds the instrumental rationality of Western lives.

Her occasional textual images throw her relentless prose into relief. The little child, sitting between the mirror and castration, contributes to her theory in brackets: *("woof-woof" says the dog, and all animals become "woof-woof")* ...

In "woof-woof," an object has been *identified*, which is to say separated out from the world. A fragment from the world has become a sign. And then all animals become "woof-woof"—the sign is generalized, becomes abstracted, the inaugurating of a concept and even of a universal.

When Julie Dowling frames the child's black face in her *Icon for a Stolen Child*, she animates the pain not only of Aboriginal children taken from their mothers but also of a generation growing up without culture and language. The "Stolen Generation" was an attempt at genocide, however unconscious and however unacknowledged by white Australia, since it was an attempt to supplant the body signs of an Aboriginal maternal/ matrix with the manufactured seeming of white Australia's lore.

In Dowling's icons, we are solicited to make direct communication again with this loss, and with this "sacred" connection between word and flesh. When the stolen children were told to forget their Aboriginal names and use only their white ones, it was from this *chora* that they were cast out. But although imbued with pathos in the Dowling image, the forgotten name is not nostalgia. It is mystery, for it joins meaning and being, the inside and the outside of the law.

Children are sacred, in the technical sense that their conception represents *life bearing meaning*, and is the literal product of social laws that mandate some copulations and forbid others.

Further, they are sacred in that reproduction of physical beings is primary to the continuation of a culture, race, or species, as evidenced by its murderous contradiction, genocide.

They are sacred in that their physical embodiment, growing up around others of their group, means they acquire the meanings of the

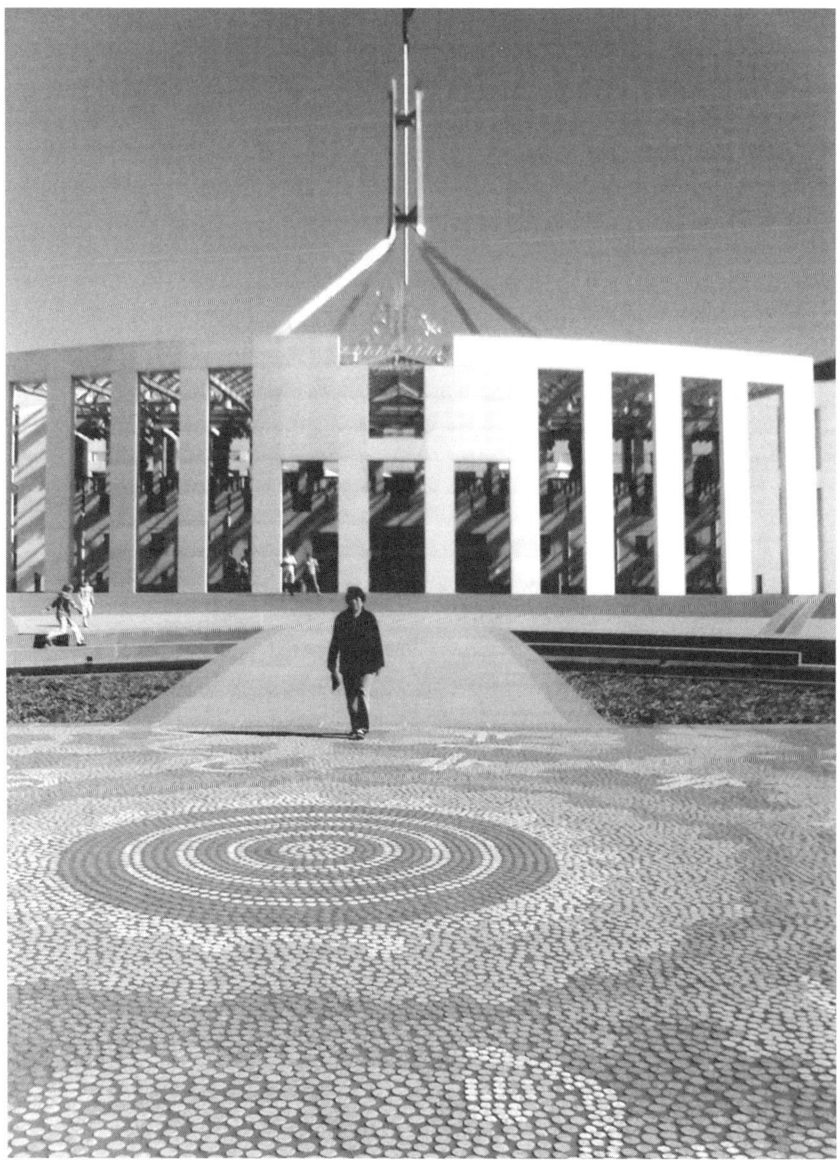

group as ways of being, and of being embodied. In accounts given by people of the "stolen generations," the memories of food-gathering and other group activities as fun underlined the pain of later separation. Indeed, that "growing up" *meant* acquiring bodily meanings that were of the group was acknowledged in the act of removing partly European children from their Aboriginal families. It was aimed at erasing that sensibility. Children are sacred, in that damage to sensibility—through violence, sexual abuse, racism, nutrition, lack of education—desecrates a culture, weakening its inherent viability.

Children are sacred in Western culture, specifically where childhood is invested with the sentiments, affects, and visions that fall outside adult rational consciousness. This includes, and is exemplified by, the mystery of maternal love, the first exception to modern economies of exchange.

Mum's the Word

In March 2008, as the first act of a new parliament, the recently elected prime minister Kevin Rudd offered an apology to the people of the "stolen generations" more than a decade after the initial report that coined the phrase.

The event of the apology was as significant in the national consciousness as the landmark case, *Mabo*, that recognized native title twenty-five years earlier. Since the *Bringing Them Home* report had been tabled in Parliament in the mid-1990s, in which the evidence was gathered of legislated removal of children from Aboriginal families through more than half a century, it had been recognized by many that *at least* an apology was owed to the people affected. The call for this symbolic act became more insistent the more the previous prime minister, John Howard, had refused to offer it.

Cynics said part of his reluctance was the prospect that acknowledging the damage done to the "stolen generations" would open the door to compensation claims. But there was also a more affective intransigence in Howard's refusal, one that needs to be accounted for in terms of the "symbolic" register of the act of apology. The "Intervention," in which no expense was to be spared addressing the conditions in remote communities that had led to the scandal of the "Little Children Are Sacred" report, was possibly more acceptable to an ideological conviction that present governments are not culpable for the policy misdeeds of the past.

Some said the "Intervention" was a classic example of wily "wedge politics" from the conservatives, who could play to the gallery of populist racism among many in the electorate while demonstrating to the international human rights community that it was actively addressing the Indigenous problems. It created a rift between those who saw the symbolism of the army coming into previously self-determining communities and those who saw the practical benefit of more doctors, more houses, and more police.

Marcia Langton, an Indigenous academic whose activism dates from the initial fights for land rights, came out in strenuous defense of the "practical" over the "symbolic." However, she was gracious in the event, testifying that the apology on the day was moving and effectual.

Of the many commentaries on the politics of the "Intervention," a pamphlet by expatriate journalist Germaine Greer, *On Rage*, published later in 2008, exemplifies the way in which these race and gender troubles have shed more heat than light. Langton succinctly, if ungenerously, summarized the essay: "Greer lays out some of the evidence of the crisis of alcohol and drug abuse, violence and suicide in the Australian indigenous population, albeit in a crude fashion. Then she attaches to this medley of statistics a few notes from randomly selected anthropological studies and proposes a universal theory of hunter-gatherer society patterns of violence. This is the foundation of what she calls black male rage" (2008b).

Langton declares that Greer is not only racist, she is "just plain wrong." Langton offers a more ambivalent view of "black male rage," which she describes in an argument sharply critical of the resistance to the intervention by some senior Aboriginal men and women, in "Trapped in the Aboriginal Reality Show" (2007).

Specifically of Greer's intervention, she argues that "the everyday suffering in communities at risk is caused by a multiplicity of factors, some originating in customary life and some in the transition to modernity, but all more complicated than Greer would have us understand" (2008).

Peter Sutton made a similar point of Greer's essay, at its publication: "The idea that people are enraged on this Tuesday because of what happened 150 years ago I think is to cast Aboriginal people as being much simpler than they really are and much less like any other human being than they really are" (2008).

Langton accuses Greer of being racist in suggesting that there is nothing these men—the victims of their own rage—can do to control their violence as things stand, since its cause is unremedied colonization. She and others point out that this is using the damage done emotionally by racist treatment and discrimination to excuse a group from personal responsibility. "One of the sustained fantasies about traditional Aboriginal society is that, until colonisation, life for Aboriginal people was peaceful and idyllic. The idea that violence—sanctioned and illicit—was the norm has been cast by the defenders of the myth as a racist misrepresentation of a noble society" (2007:154).

Langton accuses Greer of doing badly what other social scientists and historians have done better previously: "The remainder of Greer's thesis touches on issues that have been much better explained by historians, anthropologists and social scientists in a growing and critical body of literature. Intergenerational poverty, economic exclusion, lack of social capital and dysfunctional behaviours have been explored in a number of important studies" (2008).

Langton and Greer share this much: a deployment of polemic in their writing. Langton's pungent diagnoses liberate affects surrounding the intervention, beyond those of academic social science. And Greer's essay, too, is not a study; it is "opinion," journalism.

If read as polemic, what could it yield? In addressing feeling, Greer's writing can draw attention to the *affects* of colonialism, and bring them into focus. Greer's direct, even heavy-handed, language incites the passion she is calling us to reflect on—rage. Some of the strongest moments in the essay are when her blunt declamatory expression cuts through the habit of silence on pain of racism.

It is the warrant of the polemic to make outrage into a political force. Her adjuration at the end of the essay that there are *political* remedies for rage, the treaty and parliamentary representation, is centrally an operation of the genre, and its singular possibility. (How can the "objective investigator" make a demand?) Only the polemical can take us from the pain of rage to the politics of it.

Greer's credentials come as a feminist polemicist. There is much that is feminist in the insight that there could be political remedies for affects. So much of the injustice done to women has occurred in the intimate spaces of feeling. Love, fear, resentment, jealousy, shame, and compassion are all affects that play their part in the subordination of women. The feminist polemic became distilled in the slogan: "The personal is the political."

Raising the question of the sexual nature of the violence in Indigenous communities ironically can attract the charge of racism, because it appears to slander black men. But it is feminist, rather than sexist, to pursue the case of "the Black Man's Rage" into the difficult territory of the sexual exploitation of Aboriginal women by men.

In presenting gender relations as a sphere of race relations between men, black and white, Greer ventures where many an anthropological narrative has foundered (Lévi-Strauss and the exchange model of kinship, for example). And yet something in the observation of the *white* fathers of the stolen generation is necessary.

Rosemary Neill explores the same perspective when she writes: "Australians have yet to fully acknowledge how the widespread sexual use and abuse of indigenous women and girls literally spawned the stolen generations" (2002:133).

Greer, writing of the state being left "holding the baby," scoffs at the myth of these "fatherless children." It was the white man's droit du seigneur over the colonized that created the stolen generations. Drawing the prospect of the stolen generations as relating to the white man's sexuality casts it in an uncommon light. Suddenly it seems curious that the issue is characterized as one of race, rather than gender.

Greer's polemic provokes a view of an intersection or an interference—an intervention or an occlusion—that defines the events as racial exploitation when they could be as readily portrayed as sexual exploitation. This is not her conclusion; it is a consequence of her genre.

Greer's essay neither offers hope for change nor cares whether it does, Langton accuses, because the purpose of the exercise is really self-publicity. Her essay is accused of "not helping," of "not offering hope." But would all speech and writing about the political be mandated to help, to hope, or at least not to inflame?

The essay is not a study, like the literature Langton enjoins. It is not social science. A polemic is traditionally a call to arms; the genre is formed of "fighting words" aimed at galvanizing opinion. A critique may be thought to need to meet the substance, not the style of writing, except that the very style of empirical discourse—objectified, dispassionate, generalized—obscures the contradictory substance in which Western knowledge of race has formed itself.

As Rosemary Neill put it in her preface to *White Out*: "What we have is a debate at once overheated and drained of meaning; in which observing taboos is more important than exposing complex truths" (2002:x). Discursive correctness is dangerous in a political context where rights and wrongs are being disputed; dangerous because rhetorical purposes and effects vary from genre to genre, and speaker to speaker. To police expression is to exclude positions. Even more dangerous is the attempt to deny in advance the legitimacy or intelligibility of certain expressions, in a situation where *interpretation is at stake.*

"Political correctness" is social science forgetting itself, forgetting that the imposition of Western knowledge on the multifarious others of colonialism without question constitutes its mode of injustice. "These people have no title to land because they don't plant crops"; "These people have no science because they don't write things down"—all the many pronouncements of scientific discourses that have implemented colonialism.

But why does Greer write polemic about "The Black Man's Rage," instead of about "The White Man's Indifference," or even "The White Woman's Shame"? If her view of herself as an opinion-maker leads her astray, as Langton imputes, it is in the very fabric of the polemical genre that follows the flows of language into its unthought knowledge about race, sex, and other ideologies. This is the secret of how it can galvanize, by raising the ire of its audience. But at the same time, it can lead to entrenching prejudices by reinforcing their feeling.

Knowing deployment of genre, however, can create less comfortable political affects. Consider Kathleen Fallon's inspired diatribe on Australian racism, in her dramatic monologue *Paydirt* (2006)—the apology offered by the Returned Serviceman and racist father who becomes representative of a domineering generation of father figures. The monologue is spoken by the male half of the voice called "Dellkeith," husband and "pillar of the community" who is a member of the Returned Servicemen's League (RSL). The RSL has a club in every town, dedicated these days to the service of alcohol and the feeding of poker machines.

DELLKEITH's 6 PM RSL APOLOGIA

On your feet woman. Show some respect. Raise your right paw in a salute and say after me—Lest We Forget. The Spirit of Ozzie-Ozzie-Ozzie Oy-oy-oy. The Solemn Ceremony of a-bit-a-bloody-shush, a-bit-a-bloody-mum's the word, is what makes this great I-still-call-Australia-home country great . . .

. . . I'm sorry. I'm so very sorry that so many of us died stopping the slit-eyed Nips from liberating the indigenous peoples of Australia. I'm sorry that we came to this continent, when it would have been so much better to leave it to the dyke-digging Dutch or the frog-friggin French or those plonk-plastered Papist Portuguese who had such enlightened colonialisationist policies. I'm sorry that decent middle-class families committed wholesale a-similar-relationsist gendercide, that is, adopted Black kiddies as their own rather than spend their money on overseas holidays or new household appliances and leave the children to die of syphilis and leprosy and petrol-bloody-sniffing in some outback hovel somewhere. I'm sorry that misguided jurists tried to introduce justice and fair play to that amazingly advanced tribal law system that entitles someone to rape and murder the sister of anyone that may offer offence. That we put Black people in custody when all they ever did was murder, rape, assault, sell drugs, starve their children, urinate in public, dob on us to the United Nations … I'm sorry we imposed The Golden Rule—Those Who Got the Gold Make The Rules. I'm sorry. I'm sorry. I'm sorry. Bejesus you can see how flaming apologetic I can be when pushed so don't push me much bloody further.

(Paydirt pp. 95–96)

Fallon captures the violence of racism through the mechanics of humor. In comedy, much can be said at the same time as it is retracted. Fallon uses a recognizably Australian style of humor, which does violence through the vernacular, the aggression of satire. She mobilizes specific platitudes and clichés—"abit-a-bloody-shush, a-bit-a-bloody-mum's the word"—that keep familiar racist attitudes in place, and in their place.

Paydirt is a meditation on White Australia's racism. It is also brilliantly tuned to the sexist backing-choir, revealing in strings of association how racism and sexism have worked together in the popular imaginary to lend plausibility to each prejudice, and to prop each other up. In its satirical joining in the one character, whose sentiments these commonly are, racism-sexism is shown to be the *same world-view*.

The racist apologist is the white father of the stolen generations, refusing his paternity while demanding his patriarchal right. What the figure of the Returned Serviceman illustrates is the joining of racism to sexism in the one rhetorical mechanism, so that almost all of its various separate products nevertheless can be seen to profit *him*.

Crisis in Representation

Personal responsibility belongs to everyone in virtue of their humanity. Discrimination on the grounds of race breaches one's human rights because it restricts the self-determination implicit in personhood. So does discrimination restrict, or even vitiate, personal responsibility for actions?

Can one take personal responsibility for a situation not of one's making? The issue haunts not only the questions around violence in the Aboriginal communities but also the debate about apology and compensation in the broader community. Why should "we" pay monetary compensation for the acts of previous governments and previous generations? How can "I" be held responsible for violence that erupts in me because of long-term emotional damage done to my person by racism?

The "choice" model of individualism that underwrites free market capital, in which a person is imagined as a bundle of rational aims and interests that he can pursue through his own judgment and action, slams into the "cause" model of behavior, that underwrites the instrumentalism of western science, in which determinants in the history, the biology, and even the chemistry of a person overwhelmingly predispose toward a kind of character and action.

These two conceptions, the first from a subject position and the second from an object position, must necessarily compete without resolution. Specifically in the story of the "Intervention" in outback communities, these contradictions in thought undermine rationales for action.

Is "quarantining" welfare payments a patronizing denial of individual choice, or a justifiable remedy for social conditions? Is charging perpetrators of sexual abuse and domestic violence a move that lacks cultural sensitivity and fails to respect self-determination in Indigenous communities, or a proper protection of the vulnerable from social predators?

Likewise, would acknowledging land rights and paying compensation to people affected by the removal of children from their Aboriginal families appropriately acknowledge the cost of colonialism in Australia's history? Or would it place an intolerable and discriminatory burden on present-day members of a political community to right the wrongs of the past? (Gatens 2002).

"The first Australians are simply seeking relief from poverty and economic exclusion," declares Langton. The "culture wars" engendered by their predicament are an "intellectual deadend" that has "very little to do with Aboriginal people, but everything to do with white settlers positioning themselves around the central problem of their country: can a settler nation be honourable? Can history be recruited to the cause of Australian nationalism with reaching agreement with its first peoples?" (2007:161).

Langton's essay attempts to come to grips with the real consequences of this discursive dead end. For years, as she points out, the routine exposé of horrible crimes against women and children in Aboriginal communities—including accounts of the rape of babies, the murder of young children and mothers, and the intimidation and payback against those who spoke out and identified perpetrators—did not produce action. *Nothing was done.*

Nothing was done to alleviate the suffering of real people, even though the Crown prosecutor in Alice Springs declared in 1993 (in a paper given jointly to the Institute of Criminology) that about *one-third* of the Aboriginal female population in the Northern Territory is being gravely assaulted (including sexually assaulted) in a year. "The aspects of the crisis Rogers brought to public attention are undeniable and yet they are denied repeatedly by some Aboriginal men and women who ignore these issues in favour of pursuing theoretical definitions of rights" (2008a:148).

Langton writes of her disgust for those who would place the importance of an ideological position, for example, to see the self-determination of Aboriginal people and their national reconciliation, over the lives of children. The "wedge" was not of Howard's making. Langton points to "self-satisfied participants on both sides of the debate: the romantic defenders of Aboriginal 'self-determination' and the uncivil deniers of the right of Aboriginal people to coexist with settler society" (ibid.).

It is disturbing to see the collusion of the "symbolic" of a cultural renaissance against the "practical" of community care and economic development in the ongoing destruction of the Aboriginal world. The dichotomy is false; "there is a 'radical centre' in which both practical and symbolic aspects of the problem of Aboriginal under-development and its history are implicated" (2008a:156).

Further, it is Langton's disturbing suggestion that the debate failed to result in action in part because of the expectation at the heart of white Australian society that the Aboriginal is ontologically "poor, sick and forever on the verge of extinction." This racist image, which is visible in the policies and practices of even the seemingly compassionate administration, is merely a kinder face of a genocidal intent.

It is notable that the rhetoric and reality in Aboriginal communities have come apart along the fault line of gender. It is women and children who fear rape and murder; it is the male offender who pleads customary law as an all-too-routine defense against these crimes. Nanette Rogers is reported to have ceased being a public defender because she was "sick of acting for violent Aboriginal men" (ibid.:149).

The stolen generations were about Aboriginality. They are less obviously, but as poignantly, about sex and gender. The present monopoly of the issue by the discourse of race—the way that attempts to bring out its sexual perspective fall outside ordinary discourse—signals a disturbing reticence.

It is as though the scandal of sexual assault and paternity were more shameful in Australia than that of racism. It is as though the right of a man to the privacy of his domestic and sexual sphere were still jealously guarded from prying, even where that man is black. Characterizing the "intervention" as an action on Indigenous affairs seems to displace the scandal inherent in *The Little Children Are Sacred* report. Yet it is sexual abuse and violence against women and children that have caused the alarm to be raised. It would seem to be just as much a question of the welfare of women and the life of the family presently.

The marker of race does not reliably distinguish between women on this score. Forty percent of homicides in Australia are against intimates, overwhelmingly of men murdering their wives, ex-wives, girlfriends, and children. One in three Australian women will experience sexual violence in her lifetime. The violence in Indigenous communities is at the extremity of a continuum with patterns in the contemporary Australian community that implicitly condone masculine aggression, alcoholism, and sexual violence.

Against the backdrop of the high levels of sexual violence in the culture of the "real world," Greer's opining about "hunter-gatherers" *is* a distraction. A smoke screen offered to her polemics by the glib passage of affects in the ideologies of sex and race.

If proper housing, good education, secure employment, and community ties still do not guarantee a woman freedom from domestic terror, or protect her child from abuse, then is the problem in remote communities resolvable within the discursive frame of race alone?

Langton argues the vision of reconciliation is a pornographic one when pitted against the need for economic and social development in remote communities. It tends to preserve the idea of the Aboriginal as a warm cuddly creature with "culture" as his most precious possession (obviating the need for reliable income, property rights, and the protection of law.)

The role of Aboriginal art in this "screen-image" deserves critique.

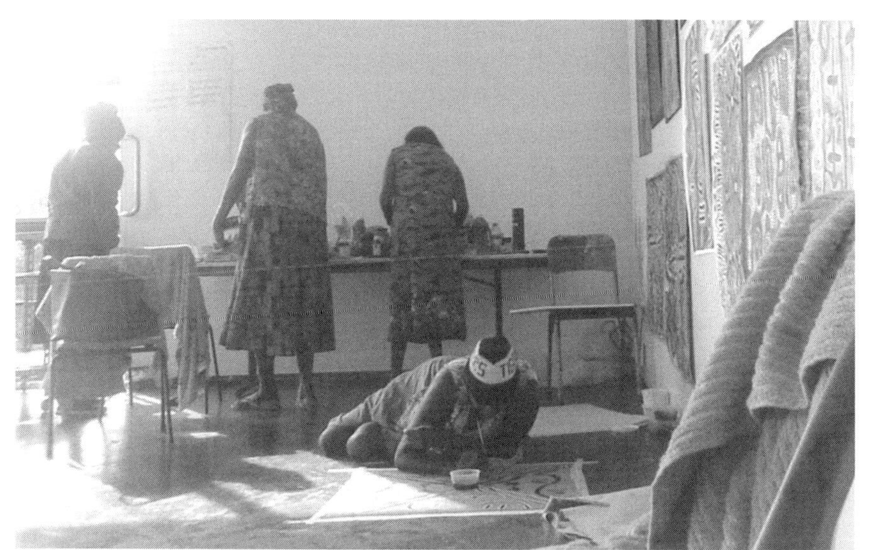

Race and Gender

The research project was called "Feminist Theory Meets Indigenous Art." When the Australian Research Council grant was announced, journalist Andrew Bolt, famous for denying the stolen generation (Neill 2002:136), mocked the title in his *Herald Sun* column.

And sober reflection could conclude that feminist theory and indigenous art *have not met* in the course of the research, except as accidental negations of each other, competitors in a similarly political project.

It is not that "race" and "gender" are now revealed to be "just discourses," words for states of affairs that here need other words. Indeed, it is the contrary—that "race" and "gender" are the names of different discursive worlds that parallel each other uncannily without ever touching.

The race debates do not capture the social predicaments that confront Aboriginal artists. Likewise, "sexism" does not bring into focus the complexities of injustice for Aboriginal women, suffering the predation of patriarchy, black and white. As mothers, wives, daughters, and nieces, as artists, the women of Aboriginal Australia may embody a meeting in theory without it ever doing them much good.

While difference provides a surface for inequality to take hold, it has not discerned the injustices arising for people disempowered relative to others. And within an order of intelligibility organized by similarity and contrast, aimed at comparison, from where can the possibilities of "real" difference take place?

No. Feminist theory only met Indigenous art in unlikely moments, in the margins of this project, when it was off-duty and unawares. But strangely enough, this alerts me to the significance of their meeting in those terms.

It has only been possible for feminist theory to meet Indigenous art along the unconscious affective lines of the sacred, through color and genre, through kids and dogs, and through incidental feelings of love and shame, anger and resentment, jealousy and disgust, including self-disgust.

The surreptitious character of this meeting really matters. In Aboriginal etiquette, you do not look someone directly in the eye if you do not know them well. When Aboriginal people are introduced, their eyes will politely drop away.

Law

Yuendumu Doors was a series of paintings of Dreamings done on the doors of the local school by Warlpiri elders, and subsequently reproduced in a publication of the Australian Institute of Aboriginal Studies (Michaels 1987). The decision to exhibit Dreaming designs for all the world to see had been a hard one for this group, who had previously protected the secrecy of their *kurruwarri*.

The Warlpiri had been among other desert groups that had fiercely resisted the Pintupi revealing of the law to nonindigenous people at Papunya in paintings. Traditionally, the display of these designs among Aboriginal people, in the right way and in specified circumstances, had legal force and economic consequences.

"To display a design is to articulate one's rights not only to the design, but to all things associated with it," writes Eric Michaels in an afterword to the publication. Further, "To see such a design, to learn about its meanings, and finally to be permitted to paint and then to display it, means to be involved in an exchange in which one must reciprocate" (1987:138).

The translation of the *kurruwarri*, formerly made as sand paintings with a ceremonial role, onto the doors of the school represented a symbolic compromise between Western and Aboriginal worlds. As *paintings,* on the virtual picture plane (and even more as photographic images published by the Australian Institute of Aboriginal Studies), the marks now take place within the global art market as art. (The doors are in the collection of the Art Gallery of South Australia). But as *doors to a school,* the designs continued their pedagogical role as bearers of the law in the Warlpiri community. And as doors, they functioned symbolically to convey their children into the Western world of written language and education, in the knowledge of their Aboriginality.

This knowledge is synonymous with the claim to Aboriginal culture, since only those who have title will have knowledge of it, and which only they will demonstrate by painting the designs. The "copyright" in designs is stricter in Aboriginal law even than in Western, since the claim to know is also a claim to title.

This is knowledge as propinquity and familiarity rather than objectivity and generality. Its performative value is part of what it means for this aesthetic to be also epistemic: "Indeed in many oral cultures, such knowledge may function like currency, and this knowledge is not 'free'" (Michaels 1987:138).

The knowledge is not free because it generates value. By far the greater part of the wealth of Aboriginal groups was held as "intellectual property" in knowledge and representation of country. A highly cerebral value-creation was mandated by the nomadic conditions of hunting and gathering, in which the means of living relied on memory, imagination, and hierarchies of symbolic exchange.

In selling the Yuendumu doors as art, the "appropriate return" on the Aboriginal artists' labor was ingeniously cashed out in the currency of a literal vehicle of knowledge: "The ultimate price for the collection would be two Toyotas," Michaels tells us, explaining:

The men who paint these pictures are, by that very act, describing their responsibility to 'care for' these places. Long ago (but within the lifetime of these painters), this caring would have included travelling to these sites to perform recurrent ritual and other actions to assure the continuity of the land and of its Dreamings. When the Warlpiri were relocated to Yuendumu, they were cut off from many of these lands, which are as far as 400 kilometres distant, and which are not necessarily accessible by road. Only Toyotas can get you there. (1987:139)

In his own Toyota, Michaels comes to learn his own epistemic claim to the land: "When I first came to Central Australia and used to drive those desert tracks by myself (before I had established relations and obligations which fill the Toyota up on any journey), the desert distances were to me unfamiliar and unmarked" (1987:142). Michaels find himself in *terra nullius* precisely because of a lack of entitlement, but his empty land was in time "filled up" with obligations and relations that simultaneously eroded the *terra nullius* and became the ground of his knowledge. It was a knowledge earned by acquaintance: "Now of course, they are a landscape full of significance—where we broke down last time, where we found Jupurrurla walking at night, where Japanangka jumped off the truck, the back way to Mt Allen, and occasionally, the place where the ancestors came, or where water is, or bush tomatoes" (Michaels 1987:142).

"But in those early days, my reflections were almost wholly abstracted." And, significantly, the abstraction he records his thoughts as dwelling on is the one that most disturbs the Western epistemology in the face of an Aboriginal propinquity later forced on him by experience. He worries about whether the land is old, or whether *it only looks old to him*. He worries that he cannot separate himself from all that he has read and heard about Central Australia, as the oldest continent, etc., so as to know what is "really" there.

But this attempt to separate the land from how one knows it actually divests one of entitlement and destroys any claim to it—and this applies to art, as well. As the art theorist, Mitchell, says, "the innocent eye is blind." This is precisely the sense in which *terra nullius* is not a claim to know anything, but rather ought to have been recognized as an admission of ignorance and as such ought to have *disqualified* from title.

For all his experience of that other knowing, Michaels cannot find the epistemology that warrants "any such ability of phenomena to communicate directly, unmediated, their history and meaning." "Rationally," he concludes—that is, *despite his contact with it*—"I have to reject the possibility" (1987:143). This is the classical impasse which arises from separating out epistemology from aesthetics, and incidentally of the mind from the body. "But I recognised that the epistemic problem raised here is precisely the one of such interest to Aboriginal philosophy, and the one which the paintings themselves attempt to bridge" (ibid.).

All knowledge shares this property of value-creation, even when it becomes part of a "free market" or a part of "academic" exchange. A clear example of this is the sinister knowledge that the "common law"—the British form of case law that Australia inherited on colonization—until recently claimed to have. It claimed the "new south land" was *terra nullius* at time of settlement.

The legal doctrine of *terra nullius* had guided Britain's conquest throughout its empire. The principle was that where the land was conquered, English common law was superimposed over any indigenous legal system, the two coexisting except where they contradicted each other—in which case the common law prevailed.

But in lands acquired by settlement that were deemed to be empty and uncivilized before the British came, the common law was transferred in toto, including founding concepts and precedents. In "knowing" the emptiness of the continent of Australia, English law also represented its own interest and produced the condition of its provenance and the wealth of its colonial possession on the model of the common law system of title to land.

The legal fiction of *terra nullius* operated in the colonies of Australia to permit the settling of the land by pastoralists without compensation,

and the setting up of towns and civic life without regard for the traditional customs of the Aboriginal people.

And because the doctrine of *terra nullius* formed part of the law of the
land, it took more than two centuries before Aboriginal people found
a place for their "native title" to the land in law. While other colonial
powers, and the British in other colonies, were obliged to forge treaties
with indigenous people in order to hold their claims in peace, no such
crisis was forced on them in Australia. To date, there is no treaty with
Aboriginal people, and no legal acknowledgment that land was taken
from them by force.

However, in 1992, the High Court of Australia in the case of *Mabo v
the State of Queensland (No. 2)* held that the common law of Australia recognized the existence of "native title." The court recognized that Aboriginal and Torres Strait Islander people may have existing rights and interests in land and waters, according to traditional laws and customs, that
the common law could give legal title to.

Eddie Mabo, an elder of the Meriam people of the Murray Islands,
and others, brought the case in relation the Island of Mer in the Torres
Strait, arguing that the Meriam people "owned" the land at common law
because they were the traditional owners of their country under Islander
law and custom.

In an earlier case, *Mabo v the State of Queensland (No. 1)*, the High Court
held that the attempt by the Queensland government to extinguish the
Meriam people's property rights breached the Commonwealth's Racial
Discrimination Act of 1975.

Mabo No. 2 went further, addressing basic premises of the Australian
common law. In overturning the doctrine of *terra nullius*, the court in fact
changed the premise on which Australia's land tenure system had been
based.

The High Court recognized that the rights of Aboriginal people and
Torres Strait Islanders to native title may survive in certain areas, and
that their native title must be treated fairly before the law with other titles.
This was a remarkable re-visioning of the law, to find that there was a

form of title that coexisted with other titles from settlement unless expressly extinguished by the Crown.

But "native title" did not confer ownership in the classic sense—it did not find that Aboriginal people had "freehold" title to country, like ordinary suburban land that allows it to be bought and sold. It did not recognize that these people had been dispossessed.

However, it found, by implication, that historical hindsight could provoke a radical reinterpretation of legal states of affairs. In addressing the question of indigenous land rights, the law necessarily encountered the question of its own sovereignty.

It is probable that the recognition of native title in *Mabo No. 2* was a consequence of the court accepting that the Meriam people cultivated their land, that is, exhibited supposedly a Western form of relation to the land. This is in contrast to earlier cases in which other, more nomadic Aboriginal relations to land were discounted (*Milirrpum v Nabalco*). This has been described as a "legally cogent half-truth," the other half remaining shrouded, as Justice Moynihan of the Queensland Supreme Court notes, in "deep mystery." Yet, divested of its spiritual-religious core, the depth and richness of Meriam cultural life evaporates. There is a certain poignancy in this reduction of the Meriam sense of existence, for to blot out the spiritual connection with the land is to cut the Meriam off from what Stanner referred to among the Aboriginal people as the "body of patent truth about the universe that no one in his right mind would have thought of bringing to the bar of proof." This he describes as the "inherent and imperishable bonds between the ancestors and the living through land and totems." (Quoted in Sharpe 1993:32)

This "bar of proof" does not survive the translation from traditional to common law, just as Michaels cannot heal the rift between his feeling of the land and his knowledge that this is an internal affair "in the eye of the beholder" and not in the "place itself."

For the Aboriginal aesthetic, it is not clear there is this "place itself," or at least that there is any other. The bonds of the past living in the present, in the land, to the Aboriginal law seems as self-evident as the objectivity of the court seems to Western eyes. While the common law must enunciate a "common law," a common vision, and put some flesh on the bones of that experience, the Dreaming knows itself to be expressing a reality—not a copy of it, much less a purely subjective expression.

The conflict that Michaels experiences, literally "on the ground," between his sense of the land as old and his very modern belief that this is an interpretation made on an inscrutable noumenon, expresses the predicament for the common law, and perhaps provides a conceptual advantage to Aboriginal law. On reflection, it is a feature of great significance that this aspect of conflict of laws comes to a crisis through questions of land. The site of knowledge is crucial to all questions of jurisdiction.

An indigenous epistemology can only be understood through aesthetics, through the manner in which art brings order to life, as sense and feeling of event. The way of knowing of the common law is not dissimilar; that is, it brings a situation to life through performance of an order, the enacting of it. Common law therefore proceeds from an aesthetic mode of epistemology, rather than a scientific one.

However, analyzed thus, this conflict of laws does not lead naturally to "reconciliation." Understanding does not necessarily produce new law, although it might. No doubt it leads to an appreciation of the difficulty of reconciling. If *terra nullius* has shown anything, it is that the force of law prevails; the conqueror has in his law an instrument of installing a real, and this obliterates other ways of being governed by other laws.

We may understand ourselves better by appreciating the aesthetic mode of the law through the example of Aboriginal Dreaming. But this will not of itself preserve the ontic of that dreaming; it will only serve to explain its unassimilable quality and why it is in real danger of losing its epistemic force.

It will take a more active interpretation to give title to the work of reconciliation.

Common Law

Uncanny congruences can be seen to emerge, between customary law and the common law. These were not the findings of the court in *Mabo No. 2*. But it seems, from the judges' dicta, that the common law also reveals itself epistemically to the initiated, in the apochryphal manner attributed to the Dreamings. In the account given in the scheme of *Mabo No. 2*, the High Court, the initiated, know the law and declare it as it materializes in its historical light.

The problem set by *Mabo No. 2* was the profound one of the entitlement of the common law to declare itself as "the law of the land." The court was thus drawn to reflect on the process of its own warrant. Writes Brennan: "In discharging its duty to declare the common law of Australia, this court is not free to adopt rules that accord with contemporary notions of justice and human rights, if their adoption would fracture the skeleton of principle which gives the body of our law its shape and internal consistency" (1993;30).

Is the Aboriginal Dreaming, which is an understanding of the land, commensurate with the skeleton-body Brennan cherishes as the law? We could imagine a likeness between the Aboriginal law, transposed from traditional sand to the postmodern commodity of canvas, and the translation of the common law from the imperialist short-sightedness to the fish-eye lens of global government and human rights. Whether this is felt as loss or as enlightenment, in both cases the law is called upon to effect a change in the landscape, to redraw the map, to make effective the now-known, to make it livable.

In so doing, the law addresses the conceptual underpinnings whereby the problems of continuity with the past and the contingency of the future are held in tension through *acts* of interpretation. Thus, "the court is even more reluctant to depart from earlier decisions of its own," and Australian law "can be modified to bring it into conformity with contemporary notions of justice and human rights, but it cannot be destroyed" (Brennan 1993:30).

Jurisprudentialist Michael Detmold has argued that difference, not similarity, should be the ground of community for the conceptual warrant of the common law: "To take the issue of *Mabo (No 2)* itself, the indigenous inhabitants desired land and the European settlers did as well. . . . Suppose you and I desire the same apple. Is this not sameness of desire? No, it is a difference. I desire that I eat the apple and you desire that you do—a difference so great that it has often led humans to war. It is only when I recognise your difference (in this case your desire for the apple) and you reciprocate that there is the possibility of community between us" (1993:40).

For this reason, he considers the court to have failed in the *Mabo* case to interpret the common law. "Whilst they recognised Aboriginal difference in the matter of a different conception of title, they imposed the European valuation of it in the matter of the conditions of its extinguishment" (1993:46).

We could go further and point out that, in the High Court's refusal to question the sovereignty of a law that was also its own source of authority, it tacitly accepts that the greater force of the conquering power gave it an overriding entitlement.

Detmold demands in his concept of common law something more principled than that the desires of the more powerful, and the self-justifying perceptions they give rise to, will underpin a legal community and the rule of law. It is nevertheless hard to imagine this view of the rule of law, attractive and idealistic as it is, answering the real position of sovereignty and contest in the postcolonial world. The law has as its first interest to act to uphold the sovereignty that empowers it.

A more pragmatic portrait of the common law has it that "the 'genius,' 'spirit' and worth of the common law is derived from its basis in human experience; its pragmatic nature; its reflection of social, economic and political considerations; its longevity and its concern with the longterm"

(Bartlett 1993:61). "The common law is merely a reflection of the society. Commentators who would suggest that a decision is not consistent with the needs of the society must carefully evaluate their rationale. The common law only reaches a decision on the basis of those considerations. If the decision is founded upon a series of previous decisions it, of course, emphasises the regard *repeatedly* given to those considerations" (ibid.).

This view does not invent the lawful as intentional, let alone as just. Richard Bartlett's view of the virtue of common law hails it as a kind of mirror: a society gets the law it deserves. The recognition of native title might represent a "triumph" for the common law, because it proves that competing interests, even between conqueror and conquered, can be represented in the law, along with the relative political-military strengths standing behind them. Native title having shown up at all as an interest at common law may show that the law not only serves the interest of the sovereign and the powerful.

But both these views, despite their differences, share an assumption that the Aboriginal case appears to challenge. Both envisage the law as the neutral space in which interests or desires are negotiated. And yet this takes no account of the epistemological task given to law, or of the way in which forms of law must have already accomplished this task in order to make any judgment in any case at all.

Terra nullius—the judgment that a land was empty—is an admission of ignorance that could paradoxically never have been a claim to land, or to the law of that land. Both the common law and the Dreamings of Aboriginal art work with another understanding of knowledge and of what knowledge entitles one to claim. Knowledge underpins the claim to title, since it is knowledge that brings to light the law, and in so doing, reveals the condition of being in relation to the land.

Perhaps the common law was not blind in the way the doctrine of *terra nullius* might first appear to make it. If it had been used to name the concept of an empty land, the land unpopulated, then it would be a seeming statement of pure racism against a dark landscape where human beings are not seen.

But the common law did not say that it saw *nobody*, only that it did not see *law*. This was the burden of the distinction between settled and conquered territory, which was held to underwrite the acquisition of the land for England. What sort of blindness was this principle of settlement? It was aesthetically blind, in the most general sense, in that it did not see what there was to see *as law, as order*.

If it could not see what was there as law-like, it was part of a general conceptual myopia that applied to its own cultural products as well. It did not (and does not) see the aesthetic as law-like. Therefore, it could not interpret as legal the encounter with a group of nomadic, spiritual cultures. Their genres, and the laws that governed them, were so far out of the artistic range of its own order, inflamed as it was by empiricism, materialism, and frankly, by avarice, that they were not recognizable as genres at all.

The blindness to the aesthetic was not a philistinism on the part of Western artistic sensibility so much as a functional part of its philosophy of empiricism, that is to say, its interpretation of what was real. Western property values were propped up on the "social contract," but this concept itself depended on the assumption of an objective world that appeared in the same way to everyone. This concept in turn could not recognize itself as a *convention*, as a way of ordering, but on the contrary, functioned as a declaration of itself as real, in a world divided by the opposition of the real and representations of it (of which language was the typical case).

We are still subject to the empirical order, in which science and technology set up an order of "fact" counterpoised to the aesthetic-ethical orders of "value." But this distinction comes under acute pressure in conceptualizing the title to land both of the native dispossessed and of the sovereign usurper precisely because "title" (like other legal concepts) is specifically intended *to make a fact of a value* in defiance of the empiricist's distinction.

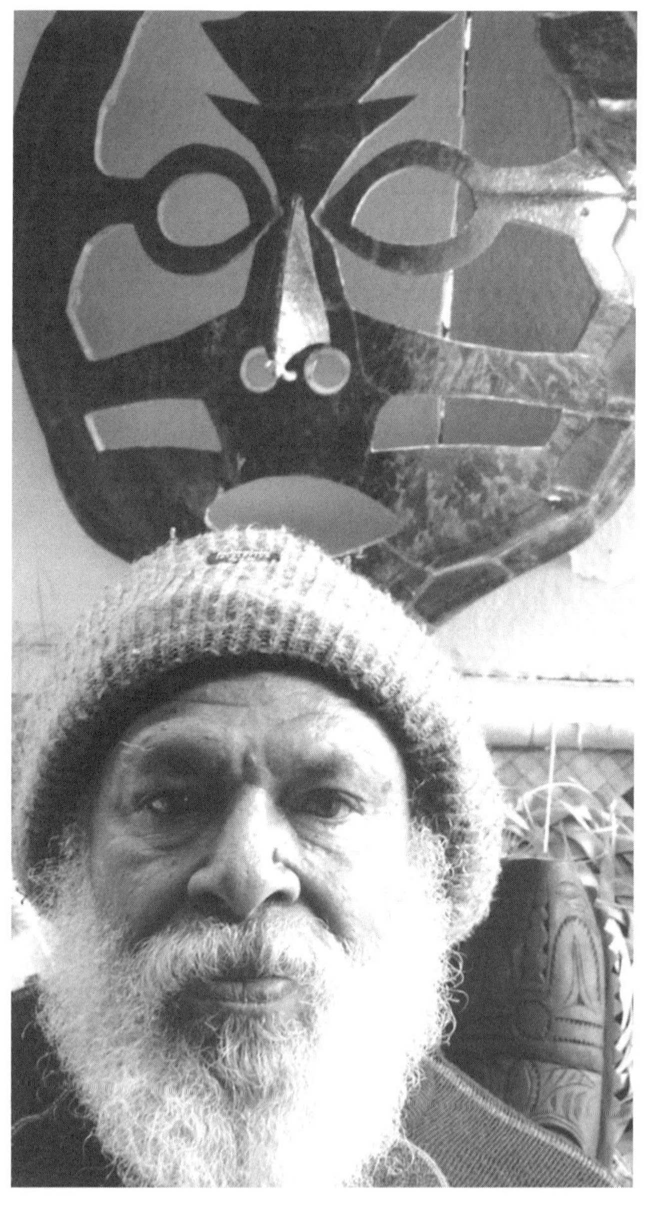

This is the epistemological action of law, which can only come about through the operation of aesthetic principles—interpretation, representation, ordering.

Meriam artist Ricardo Idagi's ceramic bust of Eddie Mabo is now in the collection of the National Gallery of Victoria. Idagi is Mabo's nephew, and a traditional owner of Murray Island.

Idagi carried a turtle shell around with him, for years after he and a mate caught it in a rock pool around the island. It was getting late and the tide was turning; the sharks were circling the turtle. Idagi was not enthusiastic, but his mate loved to eat turtle meat, so they caught it and brought it ashore, where it was cooked in its shell in the traditional manner.

Many traditions of the Torres Strait Islanders had already been swamped by other cultures when Idagi was growing up. The missionaries brought Christianity—an event still commemorated as "the Coming of the Light." They handed out floggings for those who continued the old "pagan" practices. They brought Melanesian and Polynesian influences that obscured the local ways.

Idagi learned none of his language at school on the island, only English and "creole." While he was occasionally shown the old headdresses used in ceremonies by his uncles, he was not shown how to make them. He was warned off, and told "That's the darkness. Stay in the light of Jesus Christ."

He had many times thought about that darkness, hearing "whispers in the bushes," nearly drowned out by clear voices declaring "the truth" in English. He dreamed of the turtle shell, cut and woven with feathers and shells to make a mask such as his ancestors made. He had only seen pictures of these, and the replicas made for anthropologists out of cardboard in the early part of the twentieth century.

In 2000, he was commissioned by Judith Ryan to make a large ceramic piece for the National Gallery of Victoria. He carved an urn back and front with designs patterned on the model of the masks. The piece was called *Magaram le-op*—"The Face of Magaram." When comparing themselves to Aboriginal people, the curators of the first group exhibition of Torres Strait art wrote: "Torres Strait Islanders remain faceless as well as voiceless" (1998).

Idagi went on to make the turtle shell into a mask, and his masks are now held in several national collections. Idagi's reviving of the mask is a significant artistic-political intervention. The poetics of the face is critical to the present moment of recognition of Indigenous rights.

The mask is a face—with all that calls up in us, as human. The face is the image most evocative of our ethical responsibility for each other as human. Another's face demands something of me, to recognize and respond.

Idagi's masks are not beseeching; they challenge the viewer. "What have you done to me?" "Who do you think I am?" The *Mabo* judgment declared that the traditional owners of Murray Island, like Idagi, were not invisible in whitefella law; it declared there was no *terra nullius* there. The mask is the face of that challenge: ancestors mean *history*, not prehistory. History means recognizing that there were people with a cultural place in the Torres Strait Islands long before the traders, the missionaries, the government, the tourists.

Yet Idagi had to glean his culture from books and illustrations of artifacts collected by *white* anthropologists. The dispossession this represents is vivid—not merely a disregard for tradition but a refusal of identity for its members.

The revival of cultural practices also increases the range of contemporary art. Idagi's masks challenge one to look again at the face, and question: "What is an artifact?" "What is art?"

Feeling for Justice

Idagi is active in making and exhibiting his work in order to show the Murray Islanders their traditions. To many indigenous artists, the contemporary artistic effort is about reviving the work of culture and remembering the value of traditional practices. In many cases, the desecration of culture means that the work is a reconstruction—like Idagi's masks, a strange kind of memory.

The Jewish Holocaust of World War II has become an iconic event of genocide, around which an imperative has grown. "Never forget." Marjorie Hass, in considering this command, focuses attention on what one might almost call a logical contradiction in the recent debates on "commanded memory." She does so not to vitiate the claim of a commanded memory but to ground it more securely.

The "contradiction" is this: that what we remember from our own experience we need not be commanded to remember, since we could not forget it, while what we have not experienced we cannot remember in any spontaneous sense, even if commanded, since it is not in our past.

Of course, we can remember the reports of others' experiences, just as we retain other kinds of knowledge, but we do not necessarily remember this in the way that memory is "commanded," as an urgent requirement of justice to the past. For "commanded memory" seeks an affective relation to the past, on the part of those who may not have been subjected to its violence. "What must be remembered," Hass writes, "exceeds any attempt to recall it, yet it cannot (and must not) be forgotten" (2005:2). "Memory requires that we bring the absent past into present consciousness.... But the traumatic events that are most likely to command memory are those that are also most likely to escape representation or symbolization" (2005:1).

Hass seeks an aesthetic solution to this paradox, which seems appropriate, since the aesthetic is the realm of sensibility in which these affects might be found and understood. She examines what she describes as "constructive" memory rather than "recollective" memory, as an aesthetic response that would satisfy the just claims of "commanded memory."

The possible working of this response is explored by Hass in relation to the German artist Horst Hoheisal's *Memorial Stone Archive*. In this piece, schoolchildren write letters to the Jewish children taken from their town at the time of the Holocaust. The letters are wrapped around stones and deposited in a railway trolley on the platform of the station from where the victims were transported to the camps.

Hass observes the constructing of a "form of attachment or expectation," the "cultivation of loss," in preparation for the memorializing since, as she writes, "an investment in the object must be made before the object can be experienced as lost" (2005:7). "These school children, born long after the death of those memorialised, are not maintaining or tending direct memories of those they knew or events they witnessed. Indeed, even if they are contributing to a collective form of memory, it is only by first themselves becoming aware of a current absence. By rights, the descendents of the deported Jews should be occupying desks and houses near their own" (ibid.:9).

Hass praises the *Memorial Stone Archive* for engendering loss for the past without explicit violence. "For a work of art to function as a pathway for commanded memory it must link trauma to the events of the past. Explicitly violent or graphic works may shock, but they induce remembered traces of themselves rather than of the historical loss they are meant to invoke."

It is implied in Hass's argument that trauma inhibits the production of a justice through remembrance, which is an interesting argument in the context of the "dark tourism" that has grown up around the historical locations of the Nazi camps (and cf. Bennett 2005).

Arguably, Ricardo Idagi's masks invoke a pathway for the task of engaging the trauma of the outlawed past. The suppression of traditional ways by the missionary whites was experienced as traumatic for many islanders. Being commanded to forget their traditional ways on pain of divine punishment damaged self-regard, and that contributed to the breakdown of law in communities and the escalation of alcoholism and violence.

The mask as the face of the past can "recall" people, black and white, "to themselves." For many this will be a new perception, a new questioning of identity: What is a colonial? How does that mask address *me?*

Michel Foucault argues that a court of law based on an adversarial contest before the bench has, in its very procedure for revealing truth and making knowledge, *already made* the adequation between interests that it is imagined it will discover in its deliberations (Foucault 1980:1).

To such a court, the trial by ordeal is barbarous and the opposite of just. But this is because the trial by ordeal tries *something other* than the adequation of interest. Something that we might assume is more real in that world—the value of an individual in the eyes of the Gods, perhaps.

"In my view one shouldn't start with the court as a particular form, and then go on to ask how and on what conditions there could be a people's court; one should start with popular justice, with acts of justice by the people, and go on to ask what place a court would have within this" (Foucault 1980:1). Foucault does not assume that justice and adequation are the same thing. More anarchically, Foucault does not assume that rational proceedings will issue from the people's will. "Popular justice" is a phrase of menace, allowing for a collective consciousness in which murder, paranoia, and malice are possible. Forms of judgment may be seen as revenge, arbitrary calamity, and even, simply, as an expenditure of force.

But this Dionysian view is deeply repugnant to the Maoists with whom Foucault is "in dialogue," and his point escapes the comprehension of the "leftwing intellectual" (as they function in both of these roles). The popular justice Foucault sketches is not rational, and it is not moral. Furthermore, it is not a morality built on rationality—and so is unimaginable as just.

"Judges behind a table, representing a third party standing between the people who were 'screaming for vengeance,' and the accused who were either 'guilty' or 'innocent'; an investigation to establish the 'truth' or to obtain a 'confession'; deliberation in order to find out what was 'just'; this form … imposed in an authoritarian manner" (Foucault 1980:2)—this is the antithesis of revolution, for Foucault, the irrepressible will of the people. This is the state apparatus in embryo.

And the state has interests other than those of expressing the will of the people. The state, even the democratic state, naturally takes its first loyalty to be to itself *as an apparatus.* Maintaining its own authority relies on maintaining the value of itself as a third party, which in turn means maintaining a kind of rationality in which objectivity is the ideal. Further, it requires maintaining the equation of justice with the objective outcome.

All this may be automatic to Western thinking, but it *prejudges* the question of justice completely. The fabrication of the Real World already opens out judgment through the values that are made concrete in the process.

Peter Sutton elaborates a typical Aboriginal view of justice that has no such "adequation" principle. "Aboriginal conceptions of dispute resolution focus on the regaining of equilibrium between people … what counts is not so much that an abstract idea of 'justice' is served, but that the parties severally end up 'satisfied'" (Sutton 2009:199).

In this can be discerned the staging of a different kind of law, a different sense of truth. Comprehending the conflict of laws involved in "native title" as an epistemological issue, and further, as an aesthetic one, depict the experience of truth in the courtroom or the ceremony as synthesized in that space, according to law and as a kind of order.

Apartheid

The scandal of South African law was virulently criticized in Australia, as though it were an order outside the just political life of postcolonial relations that other nations, like Australia, inhabited.

But as Marcia Langton has observed, "It is justifiable to conclude that an apartheid regime has been created wherever Aboriginal communities are quarantined by remoteness, welfare dependence, a racist criminal justice system and government officials who entrench this expensive social pathology with dysfunctional policies. The most disgusting of these is judicial leniency in sentencing Aboriginal murderers and rapists" (Langton 2007:161).

Let us take the accusation against the common law "native title" a step further. Let us "go too far" and claim that it is *unjust,* and not merely because it is "bad" law but because it embodies the essence of law. Let us accuse the *law* of racism.

Apartheid is "racism's last word" because it was the last state racism (latest, and worst, but also hopefully destined to pass into the past)—a polis built on a discrimination (Derrida 1985). In the shadow of National Socialism—Derrida notes the term "apartheid" was constituted after World War II—this institution of state power as discriminatory at its origin casts apartheid into extreme depravity in the order of all those legal, social, and religious systems that practice exclusion and subjugation of populations on the grounds of race.

Derrida does not just argue for "apartheid" as a last word in racism because it is a proper noun, describing a state of segregation, in its most abstracted and general sense (*-heid*). He argues for it as a last word in all the resonances this has with God and law, the human species as the speaking animal, a whole way of thinking in which European culture sees itself as synonymous with culture in general, and seen against a natural world. The elements of this fantasy are disingenuous but claim to found the natural order of the species of life.

In this light, the *terra nullius* of colonial law would seem to be a worrying mirror image. *Terra nullius*: an out-lawing at its foundation of any different law. *Apartheid*: an enshrining in law of an ugly difference. In both cases, law sanctifies the covert installation of power by one group over others. But whereas in the case of *terra nullius* its first move abolishes difference and demands assimilation (think of the generations of "stolen children"), in apartheid, and perhaps in "native title," the word enforces an original and unequal segregation.

"Racism is a western thing" in both these versions, and the twentieth century witnesses "the setting in the West of racism," writes Derrida (1985). Not so much because, as we like to think, we are now enlightened, or even from the demands of the "color-blind" free market, though these play their part. The setting in the West of racism is meant in the same sense as the "end of metaphysics," a "quasi-ontological" thing.

Racism and metaphysics *are* the same thing—the word, as law, is a formalization of a distinction and thus of a subordination in its very operation. This is why acts of racial violence "have to have a word"; *there is no race before signification.* So Derrida argues: As a reification of language (in its oppositional habit) metaphysics equals race equals western equals apartheid.

By extension, it also equals *terra nullius.* But here the argument pushes on us more obliquely, the force of law pressing on the contradiction on which this "West" is built. For *terra nullius* institutes the "rule of law," where apparently it was not before, i.e., the common law as an "economy of the same." Here, in theory, lies the means to a justice, through the democracy and equality it promises. And in fact, here is the contradiction through which "native title" has been able to reenter as a claim to fair treatment. But it has not reentered as the *difference* it is. To this extent, the rule of law, too, must take its share of the accusation "racist" (Ferrell:2002b).

For all that, Derrida remarks with "admiration" on the faith that Nelson Mandela, trained in English common law, holds in the rule of law. The apartheid South African law is bad law, is not law at all (ergo, it is violence) because it fails to promote this universal adequation that the rule of law venerates. By this argument (argues Derrida) Mandela can use the law against its usurpers. Perhaps this explains Mandela's success, as I am suggesting the law as adequation also explains the recognition of native title in other common law jurisdictions.

But if we needed any more proof of the quasi-ontological force of law, it could be found in the invisibility of any other law (of the Dreaming, for example) to the common law under its regime. *Terra nullius,* far from extinguished, is unveiled as the ontological practice of the West.

The law of the Meriam, "Malo's law," emphasises that you must "keep your hands to yourself," "keep your feet off another's land"; this exclusive principle found a parallel sense of property and title for Murray Islanders in English law.

The *Mabo* victory was great for the Indigenous cause. It is not as obvious how it assisted the position of Aboriginal women as women. The court was possibly reassured by the patriarchal customs of male succession, of husbanding the land and the resulting political franchise it gave men—so like English concepts.

In desert native title claims, the nomadic nonmaterial connections with country given in customary law defeated the imagination of the common law. It took legislative intervention by the Keating federal government in 1993 to bring about a radical shift in the balancing of interests between competing relations to land of Indigenous people, mining companies, and pastoralists.

And still today, a quip made from the floor at a West Australian symposium in the early 1990s would shock suburban Australia:

"My land rights will be recognized," said a woman from the Ngungar group—whose traditional country includes the most populated areas of Western Australia—"when the Housing Commission, my landlord, gives me title to my backyard."

The recognition of the existence of Aboriginal law as a "conflict of laws" is potentially ground-breaking. And yet, it can be seen in its everyday operation, to have become subverted to racism yet again. "The use of customary law as a defence by legal counsel representing Aboriginal rapists and murders is the truly offensive insult to Aboriginal culture and people," Marcia Langton writes (2007:155).

Feigned respect for customary law around issues of male privilege has depressing consequences. It challenges the viability of the next generation of Aboriginal people "where they live," that is, in their communities where, as children, they are not rescued by this "customary law" from more powerful adults around them who are under the influence of drugs, alcohol, pornography, and welfare dependence.

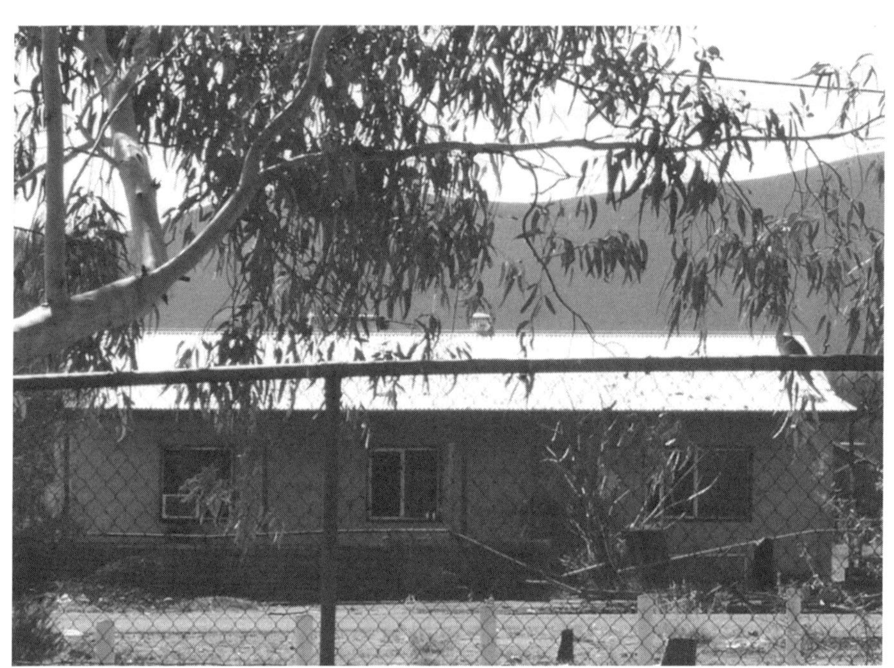

The feel-good sentiments about respecting customary law are selective. Why does it apply to allow indigenous groups to destroy themselves, but not to build themselves up (for example, as principal beneficiaries of minerals taken from their traditional country in the recent mining boom)? Why can the law be sold on canvas in New York and London but its bounty not enrich the communities in need of it?

Is the law racist? We must plead, as they do at law, "in the alternative":

Yes, the law is racist. *Terra nullius* claimed the continent of Australia was empty of law, which was a self-serving myth permitting colonization.

Yes. At various times, its protection has not extended to all Australians equally, but has aimed to destroy the "life, liberty, and pursuit of happiness" of Aboriginal cultural groups, from the massacres of the nineteenth century to the assimilation policies of the twentieth.

Yes. Even in recognizing "native title," the law distinguishes a stronger form of prevailing title that has the force of law.

Yes. In its model of judgment, the law can only promote a Western model of rationality based on the specific form of the "third party" of the court.

Yes, to the extent that the concept of law entails a violence outside it upon which it is imposed.

Yes and no. In the abstract sense, to impose law and order is to produce the intelligibility of an order. The law is inherently exclusionary but, by the same token, can produce legitimacy for ideas that are brought into the order of its sense: "Aboriginal, within the meaning of the Act…"

No. For in its aesthetic abstraction, as judgment, law produces possibilities as much as it reduces them. The "Untitled" of a work of art evokes this.

At its most abstract, ordering brings intelligibility and reality to the nascent. And so for this reason also, the law is, and is not, sexist, either. Despite the patriarchal conception of law perceived in Mabo, this "nascency" is also revealed in the encounter of two radically different orderings. From there, it would be possible to imagine a third, in which

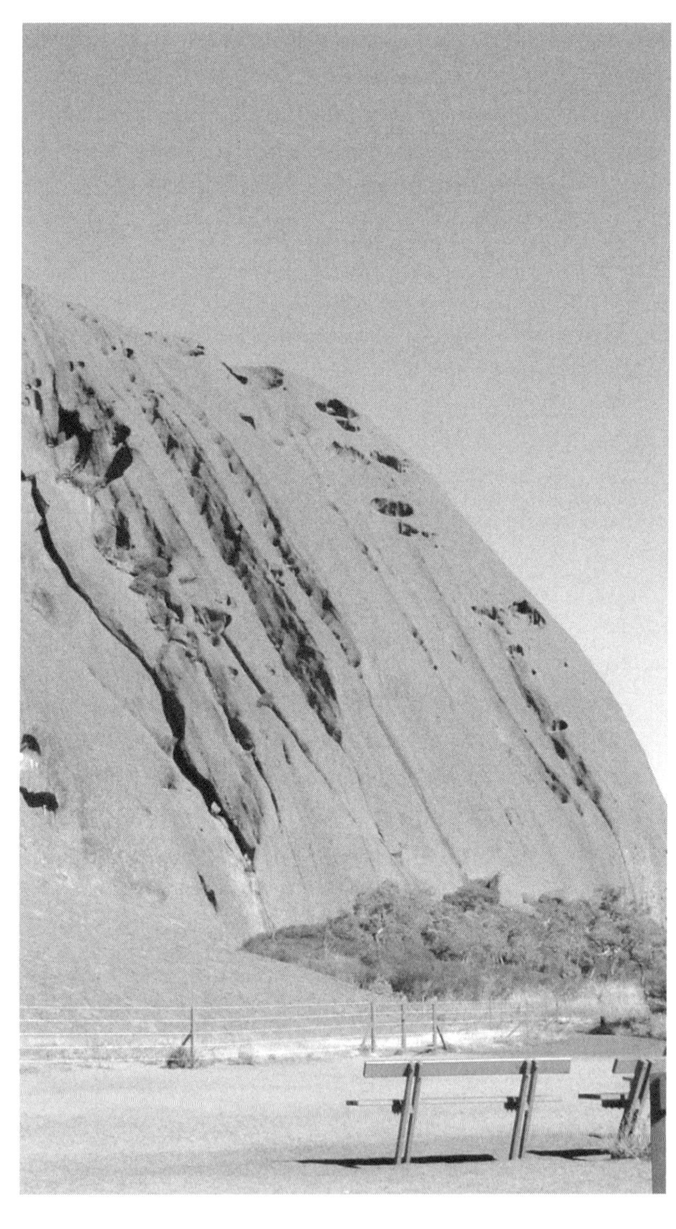

neither race nor gender was a discriminating element, a distinguishing mark.

Discovery

The rationale of the research project had been to apply the conceptual resources of phenomenology and feminist theory, especially French feminist theory, as an explanatory guide to the art.

The grant document put it this way:

> In the work of some contemporary women Central Desert artists, there is a move away from iconic representations in their painting, toward the portrayal of a more generic "dreaming." This is evidenced, for example, in the work of Kathleen Petyarre, Emily Kngwarreye and Dorothy Napangardi. Their work strikes the European eye as "abstract." However, the artists still affirm this work as the painting of their ancestral dreamings. This project will explore the character of this art and its reception, arguing it raises central questions about the difference between "art" and "politics," between ethnographic authority and art theory, and between feminine embodiment and a possible aesthetics. (Biddle and Ferrell 2004)

But at some point it emerged that the application of a theoretical discourse to an empirical object was becoming self-serving. And it also was not clear that this was the most obvious "knowledge effect" that resulted from the research event.

The grants were awarded under a program named by the Australian Research Council as the "Discovery" Grants Scheme. The word *discovery* sets the tone for an expectation of scientific-style research that will strike contemporary researchers as familiar.

It is acknowledged with frustration among those working in the arts and humanities that the model is ill-fitting. And even in the social sciences, the notion that research is a matter of "discovering" empirical facts that are lying around on the ground in the field is questioned.

But: discovering different things about the subject, surprising things about one's own assumptions, disturbing things about the whole project of research in culture—these could count as valuable "outcomes" if one could only find the paradigm, *the box on the form,* in which to justify them as investigations.

Researchers following Isabelle Stengers's analyses of scientific research (Stengers 2000) advocate a model of research that sees the making of research events as a process of negotiation between vernacular knowledge and scientific knowledge. Researchers mediate this through the objects that play their part in the research. For example, a hypothetical research event that brought feminist theory to bear on indigenous art might take as its object the sensual vitality of Aboriginal acrylic painting, just as it might the performance of traditional Aboriginal crafts such as basket-weaving now as an expression of cultural identity, or the continuing enactment of ceremony to communicate Aboriginal women's knowledge.

The pluralist knowledges of the object contributing to the research could include, on the "scientific" side, the disciplinary knowledge of anthropology, European philosophy, art history, and art theory, along with the academic discourse belonging to feminist theory and the politics of race, ethnography, and cultural studies, all of which straddle traditional academic disciplines. The Dreaming stories, songs, and practices of Aboriginal artists and their kin would also constitute a "scientific" or technical class of knowledge. In the vernacular could be included the political discourses belonging to activism around race and gender, journalism of mainstream understandings of indigenous people and culture, and the experience of living as black or white in a racist culture.

But there is a further layer of *techne* that will contribute significantly to the project, without appearing to bear on the object of the research at all. That is the bureaucratic: the administration of research funding including the terms of its granting, its detailed financial accountability requirements, and its prescription of an "ethics" through predetermined protocols. This layer will exercise a formative influence over the hypothetical research event at every stage, and the more so for being "outside" its recognized contributors of knowledge and expertise. It operates by stealth, in effect; or perhaps it could better be described as unconsciously, as *the unconscious* of such interdisciplinary research in the Real World.

Although it will be nowhere acknowledged as an input, the different requirements for attracting and deploying the funds will shape a project according to the preexisting orders of the knowledge of the West, including the commodification of that knowledge. For example, the structuring of the process in advance through the grant document will require that the project be described in such a way as to forecast, at the beginning, the outcome of the work. To know at the outset what one will find is not a priority of theoretical research, but of *risk management,* and in some ways it might be thought to inhibit research.

The schematic nature of the application format insinuates itself into all kinds of prejudgment, closing off possibilities before they can arise. Specifying aims and methodology in advance forecloses on a more hermeneutic process, and the accumulating of academic references and literature reviews nominates in advance what will count as knowledge of the object.

Ethics protocols will be dictated in advance by university committees applying preexisting guidelines. This will rule out the possibility of cultural negotiation of protocols with Aboriginal artists, and it will refuse the incorporating of any indigenous ethical practice from the outset where it contradicts the university's. This will be done in the name of scientific research, and may appropriately protect the university's reputation as a sponsor of research, but it may also eliminate an angle of inquiry that would have been instructive.

The segue around the commercial value of the research product—any paintings, performances, and artifacts produced in the course of the research, for example—will reveal tensions between the notion of the research object and the economic claim to a property right in government-funded research.

And then, the specific requirements for "financial accountability," according to university audit procedures, could make key elements of the research expenditure problematic. For example, the Aboriginal artists will be expecting to be paid in cash, but the university is not able to pay "staff" except by its payroll procedures requiring electronic funds transfers in arrears into bank accounts. And "suppliers" need to be paid on invoice with tax numbers, and reimburse expenses on detailed receipts. None of this paperwork is the cultural practice in remote Aboriginal communities.

The Aboriginal artists would naturally be accompanied by relatives and dependent children wherever they go. It may be this particular cultural context that fires the link between feminist theory and Indigenous art, mandating the prospect of reflecting on the value of maternity and family by being part of it. This will mean receiving the Aboriginal people as relatives, and with their relatives, in residential settings, and may involve the *researchers'* family in the task. Anything else will seem socially inappropriate to the Aboriginal people.

But university financial procedure will likely find it *improper* to spend research money on the "private expenses" of children, family companions, and living allowances. The issue of the handing around of cash, and paying for people not directly involved in the research, could create obstacles of a kind completely unanticipated on the face of the grant application. The cultural inappropriateness of insisting that the Aboriginal people use bank accounts, or of requiring them (or feminist theorists, for that matter) to leave their children behind, will not be anywhere evaluated. In reality, grant *administration* does not require cultural appropriateness but accountability; the research may be interpreting cultural difference, but accounting practice is not an act of interpretation—it is a matter of complying with the law.

Supposing this grant application to be successful, these intolerances will emerge through the attempt to *perform* the research. These conflicts, conducted at the subliminal level of project administration, can be large enough to disturb the credibility of the research, and create a sense of the project as problematic.

One of the disturbing discoveries of such a project may be that *it is impossible to do this kind of research* inside the framework in which it was funded, the instrumental and commodified knowledge production of the West.

Not fortuitous, or merely a matter of bad luck or the conspiring of circumstance in the event, this would be an *uncovering* of a structural "unthought" in research, the strictures of the production of intellectual capital in a global regime of value production. It will uncover *the mode of domination* by instrumental reason of its others. It will have as an outcome the recognition of how specific a form of thought instrumental reason is, and how in consequence, the Western university animates a highly specific form of life.

This *uncovering* of a structural incapacity in the way research is funded also uncovers insight into the nonmeeting of feminist theory and Indigenous art. This may seem doubly ironic, if the research was explicitly *about* feminist theory. But Indigenous art may not get that much out of it, either, it might be thought: "Since when has an article published in an academic journal done anything for Aboriginal women?" asked Jackie Huggins in "Talking Back to the White Woman" (Grossman 2003).

While the seepage of rhetoric from feminist discussions of sexual assault and domestic violence, through the social sciences to social policy-making, may have provided fuel for the ignition of the "Intervention," this is not a direct outcome, or an unequivocal one.

The traffic between the more pluralist list of knowledges generates some significant uncertainties, and this is an intriguing outcome. Did we have the task *the wrong way around*? Should we, rather, apply indigenous art to feminist theory? Such a reversal could show up the specificity of some cherished feminist suppositions about gender and entitlement, as well as questioning the self-evidence of the paradigm for remaking community in the postcolonial context.

The gaps that have opened up in the knowledge produced by the present project seem as valuable as what was learned about indigenous art and feminist theory through its missed encounter. Now *I don't know when* theoretical explanation would be feasible, when political certainty would be workable, and when ethical judgment would be desirable in this kind of research work.

Uncertain prohibitions arise for a project of this kind from at least two kinds of law. Western law raises questions of copyright to images and texts owned by other people. The question of land rights raises the issue of title and landownership in Australian law. And publicly funded research conducted in the name of a university is hung about with legal obligations to do with acquitting funds and observing antidiscrimination law, to name but two.

The prohibitions on speech, writing, and display that arise from traditional Indigenous law also bear on the research, obliquely but disturbingly, because their jurisdiction is more subtle. *Don't use the name of a person who has died; name yourself in relations with individual Aboriginal people by the nominated social relations; only some people may speak of sacred things they see and know.*

But what is forbidden and what is mandated become obscured by the way the law is relayed, through the edicts of the academy for which knowledge, too, is a property claim with significant cultural capital. Images show this at its most bald.

The traditional protocols of Aboriginal seeing and witnessing were not evolved for a world of photographs and other permanent images. It is quite possible to offend the law in displaying a photograph of an Aboriginal cultural object, person, or event even where permission has been sought and obtained, because anyone who might see it might have cause to be offended if, for example, their group regards knowledge of this kind as arcane, or if in the intervening time, somebody in the photograph has died.

Stories, songs, and marks can be shared but differently valued in various language groups, especially those that have contact with each other

(Michaels 1994). The situation is further complicated by the degree to which younger Aboriginal people are modifying their approach in the face of the ubiquity of photographic images in contemporary life.

In Aboriginal law, "seeing" can be highly contextualized, and its logistics can be unequal to the publication of photographs, for example, where the image is disseminated for the whole world to see. This highlights the cultural specificity of Western habits of looking. And underlying it, there is an assertion of a *right to see* that is harbored generally by the photograph, which exists almost as a fact of its technological prowess.

Indeed, for the Westerner, the photograph is the property of the photographer and not of the viewer, even one intimately connected to it—consider the rights of the paparazzi over the images of celebrities. The law intervenes to protect privacy, not to create a property right for the photographed subject.

Because of the photograph's realism, its probity is valued and it can originate a form of title itself. Yet, in a sense, the photograph is only ever and always stolen, its uneasy democracy insinuating itself throughout the Real World.

A clear example is presented in the case of Emily Kame Kngwarreye's celebrity. As a senior law woman of her group, she had a traditional resistance to being photographed, "an old belief that it could alienate the soul and cause it to become lost" (Neale 2008:12). Or is it an accurate fear—losing title to one's image in the realism of Western documentation? Giving yet more of oneself to be colonized?

Her market, however, demanded her photograph with each work she painted as proof of its authenticity. This is common practice in the art centers' selling procedure—because the traditional artists are illiterate, the provenance is guaranteed by being photographed with the painting. "By the end of her life, there was a plethora of photographs in the market place, more than enough to suggest that, despite her deep aversion, she had been subjected to more photo-documentation than any other 20th century artist" (ibid.).

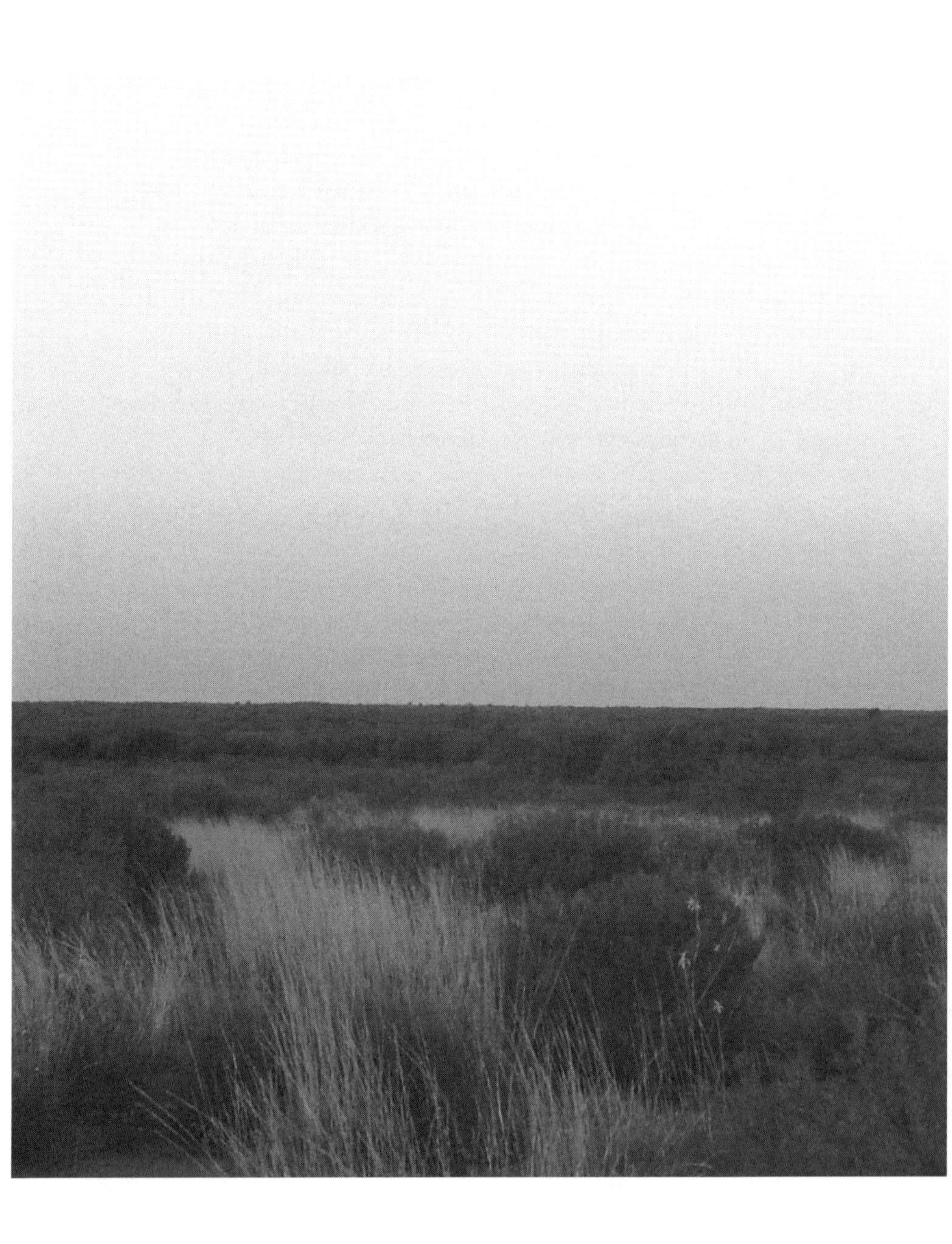

Radical Difference

In *Radical Hope: Ethics in a Time of Cultural Devastation*, Jonathan Lear applies a philosophical aesthetic to the case of the Native American Indian. In his analysis of the mission of the Crow Nation chief Plenty Coups, a polis is portrayed in which the poet is called on to instigate a *radical* order at the point when established order breaks down.

> Plenty Coups's haunting statement, "After this, nothing happened," takes on a new meaning. Plenty Coups had to acknowledge the destruction of a telos—that the old ways of living a good life were gone. And that acknowledgment involved the stark recognition that the traditional ways of structuring significance—of recognizing something as a happening—had been devastated. For Plenty Coups, this recognition was not an expression of despair; it was the only way to avoid it. One needs to recognize the destruction that has occurred if one is to move beyond it. (Lear 2006:152)

The poetic text of the dream was a vehicle by which, Lear argues, the Crow were able to project themselves into a radical future, despite their present raison d'être being extinguished. What Lear calls the "icon" of the chickadee in Crow lore is mobilized, through which it is possible for the Crow to *think* the prospect of a radically altered life, and nurture radical hope for Crow good in it, even while that good remained unimagined. "Though they faced a terrible onslaught upon their civilization, they did hold onto their precious land, and they did hold onto the possibility of transmitting their values and memories of their traditions to another generation" (ibid.:144).

A comparative study between Native American and Aboriginal culture is beyond the scope of this book. However, there is a similarity in the way the Crows' compromise is presented by Lear—giving up counting coups as warriors and becoming soldiers in the U.S. army (ibid.:154)—and the story of the Papunya painting men putting aside the secrecy of law to "give the knowledge to Canberra" (Myers 2002:5).

In both cases, the law had to be broken in order to save it; and in both cases, what it would be to save the law is obscured by the desperate times of cultural devastation.

The radical breach of law by the Papunya artists, like that of the Crow warriors, was denounced by other groups of Native Americans and Aboriginal people—the Sioux and the Warlpiri. But, at least in the case of the Papunya painting men, it forced the hand eventually of other groups who had resisted it, and appears to have provoked a creative revaluing of Aboriginal law and its future in, for example, the "recognition" of native title.

"I know the law and my paintings have law" declared Paddy Bedford, a lawman painter from the Western Australian desert. There is a comparison to make between Lear's interpretation of the Crow law of the chickadee ("listen to others, and learn from their mistakes and successes") and the way the Dreaming law takes up into itself the historical events of the antipodean settler invasion.

Take the case of the paintings of the Bedford Downs massacre, one of many that took place in the 1920s in the Kimberley region of Western Australia. Paddy Bedford—his English name was dictated by the man who was alleged to have led the massacre, station master Paddy Quilty—was born only a year or two after the event in which men of the Gija and Worla groups were lured away from the station, poisoned with strychnine, and burned on a pyre.

Paddy Bedford grew to be a senior Gija lawman, and a leading painter with the Jirrawun Arts group before his death in 2007. He worked in the "Turkey Creek" style, established in the 1970s, which included big names like Rover Thomas and Queenie Mackenzie.

Bedford painted two canvases showing the massacre story alongside other Dreaming stories of the site, the Emu and Turkey Dreaming. In so doing, Bedford takes up into law the devastation of culture, but in such a way that the settler invasion, parallelled in Lear's account as the end of Crow culture, does *not* signal the end of the Dreaming.

The group exhibition, "Blood on the Spinifex," exhibited canvases that combined the details of several historical massacres and murders with the Dreaming features of country. All announce the *continuity* of country with the violent dispossession of their way of life. The paintings represent a remarkable revivification of law in the face of the more powerful ordering of the conquering law.

It may be that these paintings, of the "hard stories" of attempted genocide, are so potent artistically because of their recasting of a politico-legal reality. By putting the massacre site *on country*, in the frame of country with the Emu and Turkey *ngarranggarni* (Gija Dreaming), these paintings insist on the power of aesthetic orderings. The men who were murdered are not forgotten even in the face of reprisals (the whitefellas involved never spoke of it, and some deny that massacres took place). These "hard stories" were performed to the Gija descendants as *joonba*, secret ceremonial dance and song. Eighty years on, they are *painted* into law. Painting on canvas becomes a legal act in a new genre.

In Bedford's canvas, *Emu Dreaming and Bedford Downs Massacre*, there is posited visually a proximity of the Dreaming story and the memorial of the modern massacre. The artist tells that the painting shows the emu, who pushed on in her march past dusk, and became trapped in the narrow gorge descending from Mount King. "The emu came along from the west and wanted us to keep going without sleep in a never-ending daytime." But the turkey stopped to make camp and sleep until daybreak, and "the turkey made the law for us to follow for life."

The emu pushes on into a relentless daylight, while the turkey camps for the night and rests. In following the turkey and not the emu, the Gija keep faith with the figure of the camp in dangerous country. In remembering the massacres, they similarly keep faith with culture. "The turkey brought sleep into existence" (Watson 2006). The turkey ensures both day and night. Meanwhile, the emu cries from the ridge, "up on top," when a Gija person dies. "She cries for people belonging to the country" (T. Oliver 2002:22).

The lawman painter locates these thoughts in visual proximity, but it remains enigmatic what manner of conjunction or disjunction this signifies in the elements of law referred to. The camp life, night following day, remains juxtaposed with a path not taken, the grief of the emu and the passage to death that she marks. The massacre site is located allegorically, as it is geographically, alongside the old forms of country that reflect on Aboriginal life and death.

In revealing these stories to nonindigenous people, in painting them and performing them, the Jirrawun artists were acting in a new historical location: a centenary of Australian law since Federation (1901); a developing cry for reconciliation in a new century; and a growing respect for the power of Aboriginal art. The law of Dreaming was carried forward into that era, by proclamation, on canvas.

Lear is concerned to portray Plenty Coups as a man of Aristotelian virtue who adopts dreaming of hope as a kind of wisdom, rather than as a wish-fulfillment. The role of the imaginative in thought is highlighted as a constituent of real success in cultural survival:

> A crucial aspect of psychological health depends on the internalization of vibrant ideals—the formation of a culturally enriched ego-ideal—in relation to which one can strive to live a rewarding life. Without such ideals, it is difficult to see what there is to live for. Many factors contribute to the alcoholism and drug abuse that plague the Indian reservations; no doubt, unemployment and poverty play crucial roles. But there is also the psychological devastation for young teenagers when they cannot find ideals worthy of internalising and making their own." (Lear 2006:140)

The argument is attractive, if in its tactful avoidance of the violence of settler invasion, threatening to become sentimental. The portrait of Coups is itself an idealization. But whose ego-ideal would it represent?

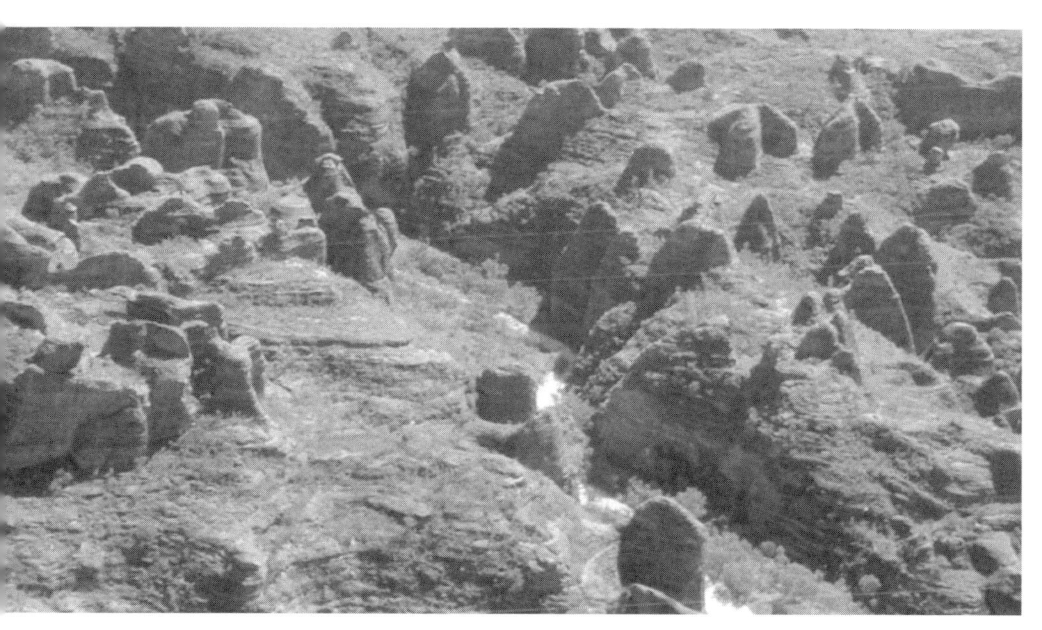

What does the carapace of Aristotle, Kant, Freud, and Heidegger offer to the Crow?

Lear's suggestion that Crow culture was more concrete than Western philosophy's, lacking an awareness of relativism, is a speck on the lens. Lear's elaboration uses the "imaginative resources" of *his* culture to outline a response that *it* ponders. More particularly, to outline a response to an ontological disaster such as the modern "subject position" itself faces. Despair and loss of meaning are the hazard of modernity, much more than that of the culture forcibly destroyed—it is arguable that modernity contains the seeds of its own despair in a way far more endemic than the structure of Crow subjectivity.

The "ego-ideal" underlying Lear's portrayal belongs to a specific line of thinking in Western philosophy, which transposed the philosophy of the Greeks into the Enlightenment of Europe, a particular philosophical narrative marked by the desolation of "the modern." As Jay Bernstein summarizes this "disenchantment of the world"—a view he attributes first to Hegel—in his study of painting and philosophy *Against Voluptuous Bodies*:

> Once there are only historical communities without determinate origins or ends, then metaphysical meaning can no longer be represented in pictorial form. Hence the primacy of philosophy and the prose character of the modern world for Hegel.
>
> So, in Hegelian terms, the disenchantment of the world meant the process of overcoming the religious enchantment of the world, with this process being accomplished once the relation of self to ground became a forever incomplete process of (communal or collective) self-grounding. (Bernstein 2006:149)

This progressive disenchantment has led not to the death of art, but to the nihilism of philosophy. According to Bernstein, "the destruction of sensuous particularity at the hand of the concept (call it reason, capital, technology)" is not "just a sociohistorical movement"; "it is about the abstraction of modernity, and hence about the categorical disposition of universal and particular governing everyday life. ... Disenchantment is real" (ibid.).

As Lear asks, "How is one to face the reality that a way of facing reality is coming to an end?" (2006:133). This outcome has already been imagined in the dreaming of postmodernity: the End of Philosophy (Heidegger), the End of History (Hegel), the End of Art (abstraction). But reports of their death have been greatly exaggerated.

The kind of reasoning Lear detects in Plenty Coups's strategies can be found in the counter-arguments of phenomenologists like Merleau-Ponty, Derrida, and Deleuze. But the "culturally enriched ego-ideal" is that of the disenchanted modern, who capitalizes Art. And the mechanism of disenchantment, Bernstein tells us, is abstraction (2006::150).

To be enchanted is to be less than rational; but to be disenchanted is not to be more reasonable. It is to be melancholy. Disenchantment is a negation that loses itself in the abstraction of the sign from its material. Which may explain the affects of loss that emanate from critical theory—the grief that something is gone, the anger that somebody took it. This, if abstract expressionism is measured by this philosophical, or more properly Hegelian, abstraction.

But if we take it up in terms of artistic abstraction, it is not so much a matter of a universal distillation from particulars, but a question of the *mode* of its reference: What is the plane on which these pictorial facts can arise?

Quoting Adorno, Bernstein, too, asks: "Artworks say that something exists in itself, without predicating anything about it" (*Aesthetic Theory* 77). Isn't this kind of frisson and intrigue released by the best Pollocks, de Koonings, Newmans—the reason why, despite everything, and implausibly, they keep mattering?" (Bernstein 2006:158)

This is in defiance of a grand narrative, of "The Death of Art," brought about by the ascendancy of instrumental reason, of technology and enlightenment, and of secularization. But perhaps it is as well to remember Lacan here as Adorno: "God is not dead, he is *unconscious.*"

The sacred has not been secularized so much as the secular has become sacralized.

Perhaps this is what Bernstein means when he says Abstract Expressionism shows we still need art. The "becoming-vulgar" of the sublime is the denial of this necessary enchantment. We attach to the world; this is our ontological mode. Hence the disenchantment is not like death so much as like toothache—a hallucination of an autonomy that has now started to cause pain.

The "vulgarity" of Abstract Expressionism "is the brightness of death that veils their bloodless febrility and clinical evacuations." The "death" in question here refers not to the explicit references to it that Rothko, but not he alone, was wont to summon into his art for the sake of profundity, but to the precise "death that belongs to the execution of the paintings themselves, their cheap colors ('a vulgar fulsomeness of reds, pinks, purples, oranges, lemons, lime greens, powder-puff whites'), their abstraction."

Bernstein seems to accept this sliding of the technical into the vernacular—vulgar has now just become poor taste, and not the abjection of the sublime that its first originality proclaimed. "Abstract expressionism invites and shoulders the burden of this promising [of meaning, of *human* happiness], becoming heroic, self-serving, self-important, fatuous, and kitsch all at the same time" (Bernstein 2006:161).

The analysis is steeped in the sadomasochistic turn of a dialectical philosophy and engages the terms *woman, cut,* and *cruelty* in the same "observation": "Authenticity without cruelty is no longer possible. De Kooning's parodic Woman is the cut of the scalpel applied with a—ghastly smile" (ibid.). "The cruelty of abstraction … The disturbance, distress, suffering of the material surface—just that—that these canvases perform (on and to us) are a way of calling back and voicing sensuous reality in its mortal coils, that hangs on nothing more than our bodily habitation of a material world in which all things pass away" (ibid.:163).

This is a religious body, the flesh of putrefaction, the bodily in its suffering and melancholy. But what of the body of delight and natality?

The body as the condition of meaning, not the negation of it? The maternal body, perhaps, the flesh of life bearing meaning, and the body of sensation not sacrifice.

In Kngwarreye, and other Desert art, one can see it on the canvas. "The brush becomes a natural extension of her arm, increasing the reach of her body" (Neale 1998:27) and recalling for the viewer "the direct experience of the body on the surface, the visible exertion" of painting.

The relationship between the eye and the hand is infinitely richer than "the eye judges and the hands execute," as Deleuze writes. The transmuting of the referent into the pictorial is only one part of its "dynamic tensions, logical reversals, and organic exchanges and substitutions" (2003:154).

Desert painting questions the "nature of the image" for Western aesthetics, and the place the image plays in the psycho-drama of the technological subject.

But the separation of "nature" from its image is a peculiarly Western metaphysical commitment. That rationality separates the subject from its objects in the image; the iconic, as a means of interpreting Aboriginal painting, is a reassertion of the technological values that have already failed it; objectifying elements of the work as images of nature, having objectified the Aboriginal world as such always already. Thus the abandoning of story in the abstraction of Desert art is a gesture both aesthetic and political.

"Whole lot, that's whole lot, *Awelye*.... That's what I paint: whole lot," related Emily Kame Kngwarreye, whenever she was asked what her painting was about, listing off the elements of that Dreaming as the subject of her paintings.

Is Desert art "imaging nature," or does the relation between the Indigenous artist and her subject suggest the cultural specificity of these concepts, of "nature" and of "image"? The philosophy implied by the Dreaming challenges the Western philosophy of the image.

The aesthetic and political question of what it would be to image nature can be *imagined* through the canvases of Desert art. The separation

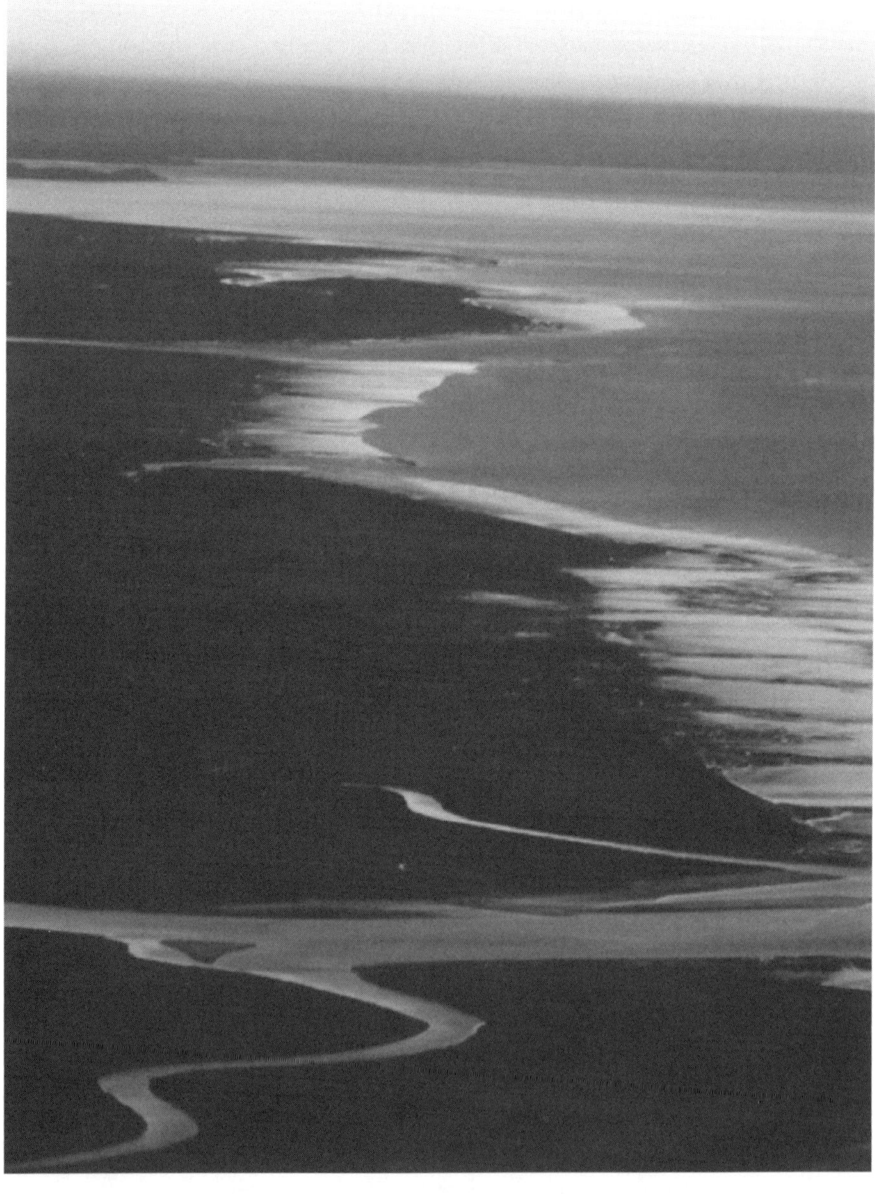

of nature from its image is the scientific commitment par excellence, and the gesture that makes it possible to think nature as an object for our purposes. It gives us the "image of nature" as an operation in thought for the production of nature as objectified, as object for our contemplation, exploitation, and protection.

Wilderness is itself a technological construction, argues anthropologist John von Sturmer, who has observed that "wilderness" would not be an Aboriginal way to think about country. "Only strangers speak of wilderness," he writes: "Wilderness is *terra nullius* in a different guise" (2009), putting in context a conflict between Green and Indigenous politics. Wilderness is not country.

Untitled (1995) shows Emily Kame Kngwarreye painting country (specifically the yam) in the insistent manner of her last couple of years, as an "all-over" vision, without top or bottom—she instructed the curator of the exhibition shown posthumously in 2008 to hang them however the context demanded. "Hers is not a view of the land, but rather an experience of it" (Neale 1998:31), writes Christopher Hodges, commenting that the appearance of multipaneled work late in her career "makes for a 'new 'Whole lot'" (ibid.:36).

It is not reducible altogether to the serial attributes prized by collectors—its rarity. Rothko's abstraction may be too pared down for Kngwarreye. According to John Lechte's account of Rothko's abstraction, "In the viewing of his paintings, Rothko insisted on two things: (1) that they were not exercises in the use of colour, and so did not refer to themselves; they were not abstract in this sense, and (2) they were not simply communicating a spiritual message—they were not self-expressive" (1995:33).

"Even if … Rothko's paintings are no longer to be grasped as an expression of something, it is also true to say that they … disclose something never seen before. This 'something' is a certain way with colour. Is colour itself essentially abstract?"

"The finite and the series evoke the author of the works. Instead of a painting before us, the notion of a finite series says that 'this is, above all, a Rothko.'"

Lechte argues it is the irreversible elements, those that could never be repeated, that permeate each work of the later Rothko. "It is not just that each work is different, for what artist does not paint individual works? Rather, Rothko paints difference" (ibid.); "Rothko's works bring uniqueness into the light through magnifying chance, contingency and irreversible time" (ibid.:34).

Lechte says of Rothko that painting "difference" in this way allows him to "put his very being into question," which is to say that the material event of each canvas challenges the relevance of the "artist" as a unifying figure behind the repetitions. Yet the author is not absent from the series, annulled by the uniqueness of each material instance, but rather is "occulted" by the ambivalence of the series, which evokes the law while it also fills the senses with the plenitude of the present.

The rhythm of *Untitled* (1995) and Kngwarreye's multipaneled canvases might be said to raise repetition in the same way. Each canvas, repeating the lawlike, nevertheless instigates a difference with each subtle variation of color and line. This is expressive of the work of Dreaming, the ontological craft given to the law in traditional Aboriginal life. It is *more* expressive of the ambiguity of repetition than Rothko's series by Lechte's argument, which is unable to unite the instances in the series except through the seemingly arbitrary geometric similarity.

Kngwarreye's canvases exhibit general qualities of the "abstract artist's" condition of work, if we use the notion of abstraction that Deleuze works with in *Francis Bacon: The Logic of Sensation*. The encounter with the painting space provokes a particular crisis of representation (the diagram), which the resulting work resolves not in the manner of a solution but in the manner of the vector, rendering the compromise of forces. "The painting exists by making present a very particular fact, which we will call the pictorial fact," "a properly pictorial ligature, which no longer tells a story and no longer represents anything but its own movement, and which makes these apparently arbitrary elements coagulate in a single continuous flow" (Deleuze 2003:60).

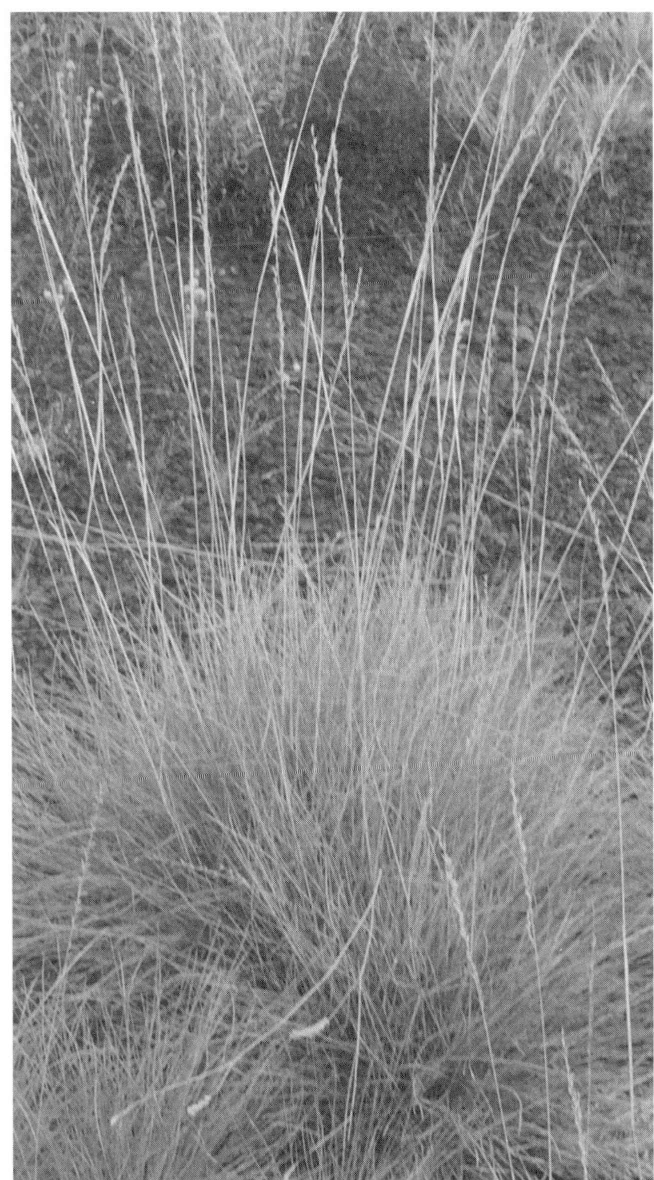

While this encounter may arise autobiographically for the artist—
for Kngwarreye it comes from the aesthetico-legal necessities of tran-
scribing Aboriginal lore into whitefella title—this does not make it
"psychological." Despite the fact that its intensity is usually perceived
through the figure of the artist, as their law, their history, their Dreaming,
the unconscious template of the paintings arises from a more objective
encounter.

This law gives the lead to its translation, and indeed it *is* its translation,
since the whole effect of it is to represent an order. But the art commu-
nicates not biographical information, but aesthetic contours comprehen-
sible for others. And what is comprehended is the *sensibility* of a certain
possible ordering.

These elements in Kngwarreye's paintings do not distinguish her work
from the postmodern—they qualify for it. They intensify our recognition
of her as an Aboriginal painter and for the proximity of her painting to
the sacred and ancestral, as embodying a knowledge of law.

Emily Inc.

To find that art meets the commodity in a circularity that began as the
fierce opposition of terms demonstrates better than much philosophy
the way that postmodernity deflated The End.

Now any opining on art really needs to be equal to the Real World
where I can buy a print of Rothko's *Untitled* and of Emily Kame Kngwarreye's
Untitled, from a museum shop or even online, and hang them side by side
without irony in the living room—and get satisfaction out of it.

In 1984, the Museum of Modern Art in New York put on the exhibition "'Primitivism' in 20th Century Art: Affinity of the Tribal and the
Modern." Terry Smith writes of it: "Could it be that the history of modernism in the arts, conventionally set out as a succession of avant-garde
transformations of European art (perpetrated above all by the attacks
of the avant-gardists not only on conventional art but also on their own

predecessors) would need substantial augmentation by due recognition of the expressive energies of its non-Western others?" (2002:39).

In New York in the 1940s, Claude Lévi-Strauss wandered, among other émigrés, in a city through which treasures of every culture flowed. The meeting of primitive and modern inspired Lévi-Strauss to reflect on what was common to all culture, and ethnography began. When Lévi-Strauss wrote of the structures of kinship or myth, he sampled anthropological observations from cultures as diverse as the North American Indian and the Papua New Guinean tribes. But it was all observed from the same perspective—a white perspective that it took its right to view so much for granted that it even imagined it was "objective" in its assessments.

Lévi-Strauss was not the only European to have found in New York a view of "the ethnographic other." Mark Rothko, too, had fled Europe at a significant time in the history of racial intolerance: another émigré in this New York "chronotope."

The vision of Abstract Expressionism, portrayed in *Farewell to an Idea* as vulgar and petty bourgeois, serves as a foil to this chronotope. It is the inverse of the grandiose but insular hero-worship that elevates the art of Rothko and the other Abstract Expressionists to the epiphany of abstraction, and Modernism to the "be-all and end-all."

In Bernstein's critique:

Clark would like a situation in which the enchantment of art and the enchantment of the commodity could be firmly distinguished. For Adorno, insofar as commodity fetishism continues to reign, then no such separation is possible. On the contrary, works of art are "in fact absolute commodities in that they are a social product that has rejected every semblance of existing for society, a semblance to which commodities otherwise cling" (AT 336). That abstract expressionism's commodity character should adhere to the vulgarity of the petty bourgeois has everything to do with this art's unique self-importance and impotence. The progress of capital has made even the bourgeoisie petty bourgeois. Vulgarity is the death's head of self-deceived bourgeois optimism." (Bernstein 164)

The debate on modernism seems "dead to the world," unconscious of other aesthetic worlds in which the world is not ending. Abstract expressionism has very little to do with Aboriginal painting, while its provenance as the last in a Western historical line is reified. However, it is the most commonly cited parallel whenever Desert art is discussed. It is the superficial association through "abstraction"—as High as Art gets—that brings Aboriginal art into capitalized Art.

Critical theory understands art as what is "left out" by technology. Whereas, on a Heideggerian argument, art is what underpins it, the aesthetic is the order of value production out of which exchange-instrumentalism-democracy emerges as one powerfully convincing mode. Its self-forgetting is a challenge to other orderings, an after-image of its spectacular production of the real. The antidote is to flip it over—the aesthetic before philosophy, and philosophy as subject to the laws of genre like any art form.

It is beyond the scope of this work to understand the psychosis of "modernism" as a Western apocalypse. But it is necessary to glance at its "banalizing" in the commodity form because it has been this ordering that has promoted Desert acrylic through a creative misunderstanding since they *look alike*.

Isn't this somehow the point? Painting is about looking and seeing; looking and seeing are cultural perceptions through and through. Philosophy cannot "correct" the impression brought on by Rothko and Pollock, Petyarre and Kngwarreye. On the contrary, the impressions they incite should "correct" philosophy.

As Rachjman observes: "For Deleuze philosophy itself becomes a practice of this abstract mixing and rearranging" (1995:16). "The question raised [for Clark] by abstract expressionism is its insistence: that we seem unable to let it go, to make it a thing of the past ... abstract expressionism appears to have a hegemonic grip over the artistic elaboration of visibility, over what belongs to the visible and what does not, over the proper and improper that belongs to perceiving, its hopes and despairs."

"Abstract expressionism is the shadow towering over the present that will not let art go forward, but keeps contemporary art stuttering" (Bernstein 148). Perhaps this is why critics and others refer to Desert art, and Kngwarreye's art particularly, in terms of Abstract Expressionism.

There is some muddled sense to Clark's bitter observation of the "vulgarity" of Abstract Expressionism. One could confirm Clark's fear of art falling into the vulgarism of commodity in the story of Kngwarreye's success—3,000 paintings in six years (there has to be some humbug here) in order to make enough money to support the community. Writes Chistopher Hodges of this phenomenon:

> By the end of 1994, while one gallery was showing stripes another across town exhibited strings of dots—and another, fields of "flowers." And yet all were painted in the same year. Kngwarreye's capacity to maintain these different styles further confirmed each as part of the greater whole and highlighted her astute skill at managing her affairs. It cannot be denied that by this time it was apparent that there was a body of formulaic work that could be described as "production line" which was recognisable, affordable and widely distributed. (Neale 1998:37)

Judith Ryan describes Kngwarreye's practice of eschewing exclusive arrangements with galleries: "The corollary of this was that Kngwarreye produced great, and sometimes less than great, art depending on the circumstances. She tailored the work produced to the specific requirements of the representative concerned" (ibid.:40).

Kngwarreye appears to have "played the field" of contemporary art in Australia. She was driven perhaps by a sense of urgency to the cultural moment, the small window of opportunity through which blackfellas might get their culture into the twentieth century.

More directly, Anne Marie Brody notes: "The fact that many works not by Emily Kngwarreye have already found their way onto the market and into collections under her name is ironic. That some of these works have been masterpieces in their own right is more so" (ibid.:20).

Remembering that Kngwarreye was a batik maker first, immersed in an artists' cooperative where the signature was not the issue, the paradoxes of her styles add to the glamour of her painting. "Although traditionally ephemeral, in reality they passed through a cultural warp into another zone where they became transformed by the gallery scene into possessions of permanent value" (Neale 2008:20). This reality arguably includes the necessity of declaring her signature as conglomerate, in effect, Emily Kame Kngwarreye Inc.

Conceding Adorno's point, that art becomes a kind of absolute commodity, it can be recast in the light of Kngwarreye and Desert art. We need to shift the focus onto the fabulous ability of the commodity, its technology, to makes things real. This art is about spinning straw into gold, about the producing of something from nothing—cultural value and the all-important monetary value for people who were locked out of the world of making things and making money, pushed aside in a place with no value, the desert, there to slowly lose their value and become extinguished.

This did not happen. Instead, from a couple of sticks—an art adviser, brushes, and a few pots of poster paint—they made a fire, and it became a wildfire they could see in New York, London, and Paris. That shows, if it shows anything, that art creates value.

But how? Not just in the fatuous sense of the market—this is an effect, not a cause, of value creation. Not even in the "market sentiment" that drives it, although the sentiment "I want it = I want to have it" underpins the force of a market in anything.

It is in the way that the aesthetic is the mode that creates an order from which value is generated. This cannot be better exemplified than in the case of the "abstract canvas."

Title is a creature of law. This in the broadest, most abstract, *aesthetic* sense: The title makes meaningful and intelligible an expression for the milieu of ordering imposed by a kind of law.

And that is why to be untitled is to be open to interpretation, free of definition—but also to be exposed to unintelligibility, to a lack of recognition, to accusations of madness and the threat of extinction.

Aboriginal acrylic art shows how the aesthetic underwrites meaning. It shows us the *real* nature of abstraction. And it shows how life gets caught in the machinery of meaning. The canvas becomes a deus ex machina, necessarily mysterious, obliged to disguise its creation. Hence it is a *mystery*.

The Desert paintings carry that mystery into the Real World, as vitality, as glamour in the old sense of a spell. They carry forward the inconsistencies, atrocities, misunderstandings, and omissions as their genesis, in their charisma.

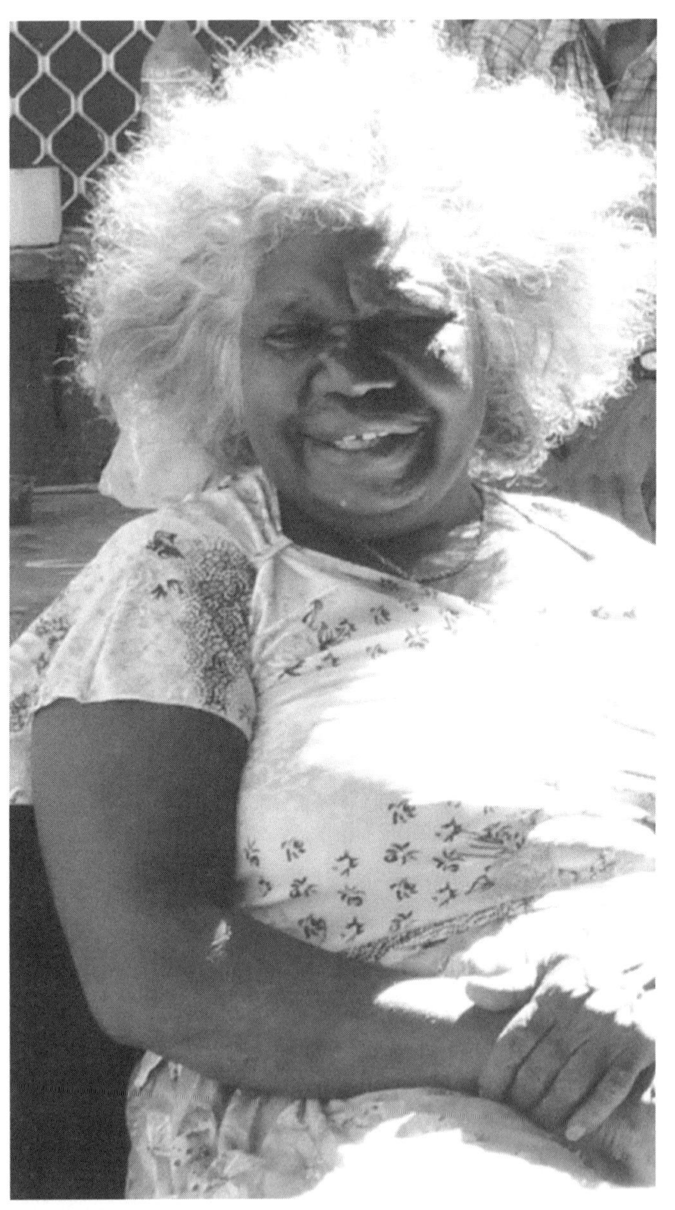

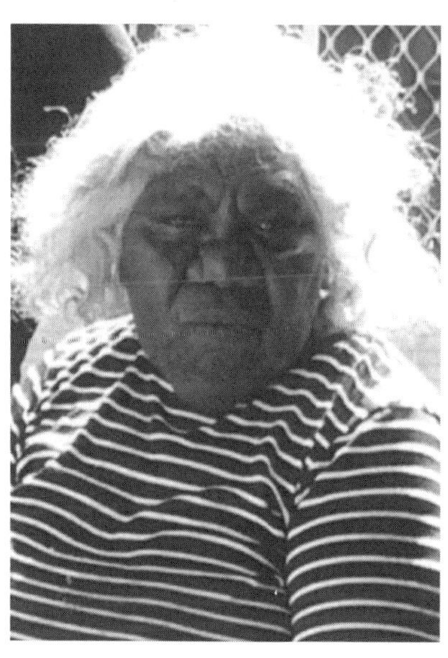

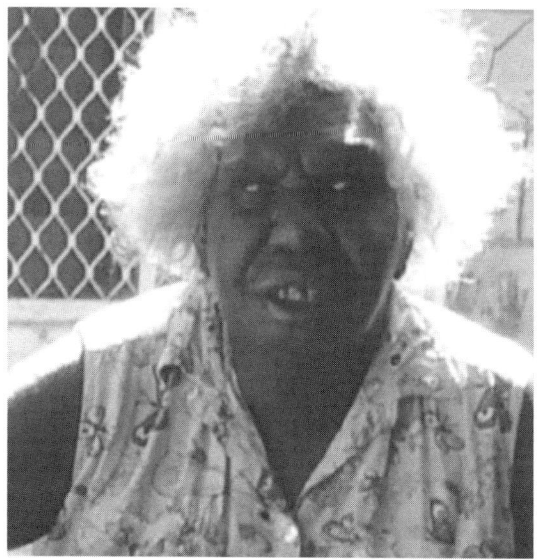

Andrew, Brook. 2008. Theme Park Catalog. Utrecht: AAMU.

Bardon, Geoffrey. 2004. *Papunya: A Place Made after the Story*. Melbourne: Melbourne University Press.

Barthes, Roland. 1981. *Camera Lucida*. New York: Hill and Wang.

———. 1982. Susan Sontag, ed. *A Barthes Reader*. New York: Hill and Wang.

Bartlett, Richard. 1993. "Aboriginal Law Does Now Run in Australia." In *Essays on the Mabo Decision*. Sydney: Law Book Co.

Battersby, Christine. 1989. *Gender and Genius: Towards a Feminist Aesthetics*. London: Women's Press.

Benjamin, Walter. 1996. *Selected Writings 1913-26*. Marius Bullock and Michael V. Jennings (eds). Vol. 1. Cambridge, Mass.: Harvard University Press.

Bennett, Jill. 2005. "The Dynamics of Resonance." *South: Australian and New Zealand Journal of Art* 6:2–7:1.

Bernstein, J. M. 2006. *Against Voluptuous Bodies: Late Modernism and the Meaning of Painting*. Palo Alto: Stanford University Press.

Bersani, Leo. 1986. *The Freudian Body: Psychoanalysis and Art*. New York: Columbia University Press.

Biddle, Jennifer. 1991. "Dot, Circle, Difference: Translating Central Desert Paintings." In *Cartographies: Poststructuralism and the Mapping of Bodies and Spaces*, ed. Rosalyn Diprose and Robyn Ferrell, pp. 27–39. St. Leonards, Sydney: Allen and Unwin.

————. 2007. *Breast Bodies Canvas*. Sydney: University of New South Wales Press.

Biddle, Jennifer, and Robyn Ferrell. 2004. ARC Discovery Grant Application DP0558842 (unpublished).

Borradori, Giovanna. 2003. *Philosophy in a Time of Terror: Dialogues with Jurgen Habermas and Jacques Derrida*. Chicago and London: University of Chicago Press.

Brennan, Frank. 1993. " 'The Consent of the Natives': Mabo and Indigenous Political Rights." In *Essays on the Mabo Decision*. Sydney: Law Book Co.

"Bringing Them Home." 1996. Report into the stolen generations.

Chanter, Tina. 2007. *The Picture of Abjection: Film, Fetish, and the Nature of Difference*. Bloomington: Indiana University Press.

Clément, Catherine. 2006. *Qu'est-ce qu'un peuple premier?* Paris: Editions du Panama.

Clifford, James, and Marcus, George E. (eds). 1986. *Writing Culture: The Poetics and Politics of Ethnography*. Berkeley: University of California Press.

————. 1988. *The Predicament of Culture: Twentieth-Century Ethnography, Literature, and Art*. Cambridge, Mass.: Harvard University Press.

Cubilié, Anne. 2005. *Women Witnessing Terror: Testimony and the Cultural Politics of Human Rights*. New York: Fordham University Press.

Deger, Jennifer. 2006. *Shimmering Screens: Making Media in an Aboriginal Community*. Minneapolis: University of Minnesota Press.

Deleuze, Gilles. 2003. *Francis Bacon: The Logic of Sensation*. Daniel W. Smith, trans. London: Verso.

Derrida, Jacques. 1985. "Racism's Last Word." *Critical Inquiry* 12:290–99.

————. 1987a. *The Truth in Painting*. Geoffrey Bennington and Ian McLeod, trans. Chicago: University of Chicago Press.

————.1987b. *For Nelson Mandela*. New York: Seaver (*Pour Nelson Mandela*, 1986 Editions Gallimard).

————. 1992. "The Law of Genre." In *Acts of Literature*, ed. Derek Attridge. New York: Routledge.

Detmold, Michael. 1993. "Australians and Aborigines and the Mabo Decision: Just Who Needs Whom the Most?" In *Essays on the Mabo Decision*. Sydney: Law Book Co.

Dibley, Ben. 2007. "Antipodean Aesthetics, Public Policy and the Museum." In *Cultural Studies Review* 13 (1) (March).

Diprose, Rosalyn. 1994. *The Bodies of Women: Ethics, Embodiment and Sexual Difference.* London and New York: Routledge.

————. 2006. "The Art of Dreaming: Merleau-Ponty and Petyarre on Flesh Expressing a World." In *Cultural Studies Review* 12 (1) (March).

Fallon, Kathleen Mary. 2006. *Paydirt.* Crawley: University of Western Australia Press.

Ferrell, Robyn. 1996. *Passion in Theory.* London: Routledge.

————. 2002. *Genres of Philosophy.* Aldershot, UK: Ashgate.

————. 2003. "Untitled: Art as Law," *Studies in Practical Philosophy* 3(1), 38–52.

————. 2003a. "Pinjarra 1970." *Cultural Studies Review* 9(1), 23–34.

————. 2007. "Translating Worlds: Is Petyarre's Work Abstract?" *Cultural Studies Review* 13(1), 121-28.

Foucault, Michel. 1980. *Power/Knowledge: Selected Interviews and Other Writings, 1972–1977.* Colin Gordon, ed. Hemel Hempstead: Harvester Press.

Freud, Sigmund. 1900. *The Interpretation of Dreams.* James Strachey, ed.. Standard Edition vols. 4 and 5. Hogarth Press.

Gage, John. 1993. *Colour and Culture: Practice and Meaning from Antiquity to Abstraction.* London: Thames and Hudson.

————. 1999. *Colour and Meaning: Art, Science and Symbolism.* London: Thames and Hudson.

Gatens, Moira. 1996. *Imaginary Bodies: Ethics, Power and Corporeality.* London: Routledge.

————. 2002. "Post-Colonialism and History: Are We Responsible for the Past?" In *Extreme Beauty: Aesthetics, Politics, Death,* ed. James Swearingen and Joanne Cutting-Gray. New York and London: Continuum.

Genocchio, Benjamin. 2008. *Dollar Dreaming: Inside the Aboriginal Art World.* Melbourne: Hardie Grant.

Greer, Germaine. 2008. *On Rage.* Melbourne: Melbourne University Press.

Grossman, Michele, ed. 2003. *Blacklines: Contemporary Critical Writing by Indigenous Australians.* Melbourne: University of Melbourne Press.

Harrison, Charles, and Paul Wood, eds. 2003. *Art in Theory, 1900–2000: An Anthology of Changing Ideas.* 2nd Edition. Oxford: Blackwell.

Hass, Marjorie. 2005. "Never Forget: An Aesthetics of Commanded Memory." Paper delivered to the American Philosophical Association Convention, Chicago.

Hawthorne, Susan, and Bronwyn Winter. 2003. *After Shock: September 11, 2001: Global Feminist Perspectives.* Vancouver: Raincoast Books.

Heidegger, Martin. 1977. *Basic Writings*. David Farrell Krell, ed. New York: Harper and Row.

hooks, bell. 1990. *Yearning: Race, Gender, and Cultural Politics*. Cambridge, Mass.: South End Press.

Indigenous Studies Program. 2007. Agreements, Treaties and Negotiated Settlements Project on-line database: University of Melbourne.

James, Stanley M., and Claire C. Robertson, eds. 2005. *Genital Cutting and Transnational Sisterhood: Disputing U.S. Polemics*. Urbana and Chicago: University of Illinois Press.

Johnson, Vivien. 1996. *Copyrites: Aboriginal Art in the Age of Reproductive Technologies*. Sydney: National Indigenous Arts Advocacy Association and Macquarie University.

————, ed. 2007. *Papunya Painting: Out of the Desert*. Canberra: National Museum of Australia.

————. 2010. *Once Upon a Time in Papunya*. Sydney: University of NSW Press.

Kobré, Ken. 2004. *Photojournalism: The Professionals' Approach*. 5th Edition, Betsy Brill, ed. Focal Press.

Kristeva, Julia. 1984. *Revolution in Poetic Language*. New York: Columbia University Press.

————. 1987. *In the Beginning Was Love: Psychoanalysis and Faith*. Arthur Goldhammer, trans. New York: Columbia University Press.

————. 1989. *Language: The Unknown*. Anne M. Menke, trans. New York: Columbia University Press.

————. 1991. *Strangers to Ourselves*. Leon Roudiez, trans. New York: Columbia University Press.

————. 1995. *New Maladies of the Soul*. Ross Guberman, trans. New York: Columbia University Press.

————, and Catherine Clément. 2001. *The Feminine and the Sacred*. New York: Columbia University Press.

Langton, Marcia. 1993. *"Well, I Heard It on the Radio and I Saw It on the Television . . .": An Essay for the Australian Film Commission on the Politics and Aesthetics of Filmmaking by and about Aboriginal People and Things*. North Sydney: Australian Film Commission.

————. 2007. "Trapped in the Aboriginal Reality Show." *Griffith Review* 19: Re-Imagining Australia, ed. Julianne Schulz (Autumn):143–62.

———. 2008. "Germaine Greer's Essay Is Racist: Marcia Langton." *The Australian*, August 19.

Lear, Jonathan. 2006. *Radical Hope: Ethics in the Face of Cultural Devastation*. Cambridge, Mass., and London: Harvard University Press.

Lechte, John. "Thinking the Reality of Abstraction." In *Abstraction: A Journal of Philosophy and the Visual Arts*, no. 5, p. 33.

"Little Children are Sacred." 2007. Report to the Northern Territory Government.

Mabo No. 2 [1992] 175 CLR 1; 66 ALJR 408; 107 ALR 1.

Mellor, Doreen, and Anna Haebich. 2002. *Many Voices: Reflections on Experiences of Indigenous Child Separation*. Canberra: National Library of Australia.

Merleau-Ponty, Maurice. 1962. *The Phenomenology of Perception*. Colin Smith, trans. London: Routledge and Kegan Paul.

———. 1968. *The Visible and the Invisible*. Alphonso Lingis, trans. Evanston, Ill.: Northwestern University Press.

———. 1973. *"Expression and the Child's Drawing" in The Prose of the World*. John O'Neill, trans. Chicago: Northwestern University Press.

Michaels, Eric. 1987. Foreword to *Kurruwarri: Yuendumu Doors*. Canberra: Australian Institute of Aboriginal Studies.

———. 1994. *Bad Aboriginal Art: Tradition, Media, and Technological Horizons*. Minneapolis: University of Minnesota Press and Sydney: Allen and Unwin.

Milirrpum v Nabalco [1971] 17 FLR 141; [1972–73] ALR 65.

Morphy, Howard. 1991. *Ancestral Connections: Art and an Aboriginal System of Knowledge*. Chicago: University of Chicago Press.

———. 1998. *Aboriginal Art*. London: Phaidon.

———. 2008. *Becoming Art: Exploring Cross-Cultural Categories*. Sydney: University of New South Wales Press.

Mosby, Tom. 1998. "Ilan Pasim (This Is Our Way): Torres Strait Art." Cairns: Cairns Regional Gallery.

Muecke, Stephen. 1998. *No Road: Bitumen All the Way*. Fremantle: Fremantle Arts Centre Press.

Myers, Fred. 2002. *Painting Culture: The Making of an Aboriginal High Art*. Durham, N.C. and London: Duke University Press.

National Gallery of Victoria. 2006. *Landmarks* exhibition catalog.

———. 2008. *Across the Desert: Aboriginal Batik from Central Australia*. Exhibition and catalog.

Neale, Margo. 1998. *Emily Kame Kngwarreye: Alhalkere: Paintings from Utopia*. Melbourne: Macmillan.

———. 2008 (ed). *Utopia: The Genius of Emily Kame Kngwarreye*. Canberra: National Museum of Australia Press.

Neill, Rosemary. 2002. *White Out*. Sydney: Allen and Unwin.

Nicholls, Christine, and Ian North. 2001. *Kathleen Petyarre: Genius of Place*. Kentown: Wakefield Press.

Oliver, Kelly. 2004. *The Colonization of Psychic Space: A Psychoanalytic Social Theory of Oppression*. Minneapolis: University of Minnesota Press.

Oliver, Kelly, and Keltner, S. K. (eds). 2009. *Psychoanalysis, Aesthetics, and Politics in the Work of Julia Kristeva*. Albany: State University of New York Press.

Oliver, Tony, ed. 2002. *Blood on the Spinifex*. Catalog of exhibition at Ian Potter Gallery, Melbourne.

Perkins, Hetti, and Margie West, eds. 2007. *One Sun One Moon: Aboriginal Art in Australia*. Sydney: Art Gallery of New South Wales.

Price, Rebecca, and Elizabeth Nicholson, eds. 2006. *Dreaming Their Way*. Washington, D.C.: National Museum of Women in the Arts.

Rachjman, John. 1995. "Another View of Abstraction." In *Abstraction: A Journal of Philosophy and the Visual Arts* no. 5, 16-23.

Reilly, Patricia. 1992. "The Taming of the Blue: Writing Out Color in Italian Renaissance Theory." In *The Expanding Discourse: Feminism and Art History*, ed. Norma Broude and Mary Garrard. New York: HarperCollins.

Rothwell, Nicolas. 2007. *Another Country*. Melbourne: Black Inc.

Ryan, Judith. 1989. *Mythscapes: Aboriginal Art of the Desert*. Melbourne: National Gallery of Victoria.

———. 1993. *Images of Power: Aboriginal Art from the Kimberley* (with Kim Ackerman). Melbourne: National Gallery of Victoria.

———. 2004. *Colour Power: Aboriginal Art Post 1984*. Melbourne: National Gallery of Victoria.

Sharpe, Noni. 1993. "Law and Difference: Reflections on Mabo's Case." In *Essays on the Mabo Decision*. Sydney: Law Book Co.

Silverman, Kaja. 1996. *The Threshold of the Visible World*. London and New York: Routledge.

Skelton, Russell. 2010. *King Brown Country: The Betrayal of Papunya.* Sydney: Allen and Unwin.

Smith, Terry. 2002. *Transformations in Australian Art.* vol. 2: *The 20th Century—Modernism and Aboriginality.* Sydney: Thames and Hudson.

————. 2008. "Creating Value Between Cultures: Contemporary Aboriginal Art." In *Beyond Price: Values and Valuing in Art and Culture,* ed. Michael Hütter and David Throsby. Cambridge: Cambridge University Press.

Sontag, Susan. 2003. *Regarding the Pain of Others.* New York: Farrar, Straus and Giroux.

Stengers, Isabelle. 2000. *The Invention of Modern Science.* Daniel W. Smith, trans. Minneapolis: University of Minnesota Press.

Sturmer, John von. 2009. *When the Image Looks Back* (download). Melbourne: Institute of Postcolonial Studies.

Sullivan, Shannon. 2006. *Revealing Whiteness: The Unconscious Habits of Racial Privilege.* Bloomington: Indiana University Press.

Sutton, Peter, ed. 1988. *Dreamings: The Art of Aboriginal Australia.* New York and Ringwood: Viking, in Association with the Asia Societies Gallery.

————. 2008. Interview with 7.30 Report ABC Television, September.

————. 2009. *The Politics of Suffering.* Melbourne: Melbourne University Press.

Tate Gallery. 1987. *Mark Rothko: 1903–1970.* London.Watson, Ken. 2006. Paddy Bedford download to accompany national touring exhibition. Sydney: Museum of Contemporary Art.

Weiss, Gail. 1999. *Body Images: Embodiment as Intercorporeality.* London and New York: Routledge.

Wright, Felicity. 2000. *The Art & Craft Centre Story.* Volume 2: *Summary and Recommendations.* Canberra: Aboriginal and Torres Strait Islander Commission.

Young, Diana. 2007. "The Invention of Colour." Unpublished paper presented to "Beyond Text?" conference, University of Manchester.

Ziarek, Ewa. 2001. *An Ethics of Dissensus: Feminism, Postmodernity, and the Politics of Radical Democracy.* Stanford, Calif.: Stanford University Press.

AAMU museum for contemporary Aboriginal Art, 46

Aboriginal art: abstraction and, 17–19, 139, 141–142, 144, 146–149; art history and, 55–56; "carpetbagging" and, 47, 49; colonial history and, 13; color and, 19–21, 23, 25, 26–27; discovery process and, 124; feminism and feminist theory, 96–97, 123–129; law and, 99–105; origins of acrylic painting genre, 27–28, 30–33, 35, 37–43; political demands and, 2; sacredness and, 5; tourist merchandise and, 36; Western worldview and, 62, 64. *See also* acrylic painting

Aboriginal culture: assimilationist policies and, 49–50, 52; gender and, 76–77, 79; Germaine Greer and, 85–89; housing, 120; living standards and, 46; personal responsibility and, 92–94

Abstract Expressionism, 17, 137, 138, 145–147

abstraction: Aboriginal art and, 15, 16, 17–19; art as a commodity and, 144–149; art theory and, 1, 2; color and, 22–23; "country" and landscape, 101–102; disenchantment and, 137; law and, 121, 123; Mark Rothko, 141–142; origins of acrylic painting genre, 31

acrylic painting, 48; Aboriginal art and, 2–3, 13, 15; color and, 19–20; End of Art theory and, 1; origins of genre, 27–28, 30–33, 35, 37–43; Utopia, Australia, 7, 8

"adequation" principle, 115, 116

Adorno, Theodor W., 137–138, 148

adult education. *See* art education

advertising images, 64–65

aesthetics: Aboriginal art and, 13, 15, 104–105; customary law and, 109; Dreaming and, 12–13; ethics and, 2; "Real World" and, 3–5; semiotics and, 59–60. *See also* Western aesthetics

affective movements, 26–27

agriculture, land claims and, 104

altyerrenge (Dreamtime), 8–9
ancestral beings, 12
anthropology, study of, 42–43, 124
apartheid, 116–119, 121, 123
apologies, from Australian government,
    84–85, 91
appearance, of art, 146
Armstrong, Agnes, 150
art appreciation, 55, 60, 66, 68
art centers. *See* community art initiatives
art criticism, 43, 47
art education, 28, 30, 31–32
"art for art's sake," 39–40, 52–53
Art Gallery of New South Wales, 55–56
art history, museums and, 55–56
artifacts, 55–56, 112
artist, career as, 7–8
artistic judgments, 38
art materials, 30, 31–32, 54, 60
"art of the other," 39
art theory: abstraction and, 2, 18–19,
    101–102, 146; artistic representation
    and, 1
assimilationist policies, 33, 35, 49–50,
    77, 79
audiences, museums and, 52–56
Australian art community, 64
authenticity, of art pieces, 148

Bad Aboriginal Art (Michaels), 38
Balinese batik designs, 28
Bardon, Geoff, 30, 31–32, 33, 35
Barthes, Roland, 68–69, 70
Bartlett, Richard, 107–108
batik designs, 13, 27–28, 29
beauty, of art, 50
Bedford, Paddy, 25, 132, 133–134
Bedford Downs massacre, 132–133

Bell, Richard, 62
Benjamin, Walter, 58, 59
Bernstein, Jay, 136–138, 145–146
Biddle, Jennifer, 12–13, 52, 75, 76
biographical information, art and, 144
"blockbuster" exhibitions, museums
    and, 54–55
"Blood on the Spinifex" exhibition, 133
blue, color of, 25
bodies: Abstract Expressionism, 138–139;
    language and, 80, 81
body art, 12
Bolt, Andrew, 96
Brennan, Frank, 106
Brody, Anne Marie, 148
Byzantine art, 71, 80–81

camp dogs, 34
"carpetbagging," 47, 49
Carter, Kevin, 71–72
ceremonial activities, 13, 39, 75, 99–100
Cézanne, Paul, 22
child abuse, 49, 76–77, 87–88, 92–94
children, sacredness of, 79–82, 84
Christianity, 111
Clifford, James, 4, 56
collaborative artworks, 38–39, 148
collecting, museums and, 56
College of Fine Arts, Sydney, 95
colonialism: Aboriginal art and, 13;
    Abstract Expressionism and, 17;
    cultural genocide and, 33, 35; origins
    of acrylic painting genre, 32–33;
    political correctness and, 88–89
color: Aboriginal art and, 19–21, 23, 25,
    26–27; Abstract Expressionism and,
    138; Mark Rothko, 142; origins of
    acrylic painting genre, 32; psychology

of, 25–26; Western aesthetics and,
    21–23

Color and Meaning (Gage), 26

colore-disegno opposition, 21–22, 23, 25

color theory, 21, 23, 26

"color without theory," 22, 23

"commanded memory," 113–114

commercial art, 32, 37

commodities: art as, 54–55, 71, 144–149;
    research products as, 125–126

common law, 106–109, 111–112; apartheid
    and, 117, 118; "country" and landscape,
    105; customary law and, 119; racism
    and, 121; *terra nullius* legal doctrine and,
    102–103

communication, translation and, 58–60,
    62

community art initiatives, 31, 37–38, 47

community standards, child abuse
    and, 49

compensation, 91, 92

constructive memory, 113–114

contemporary art: Aboriginal art and, 13,
    25, 41, 46; Abstract Expressionism, 17;
    origins of acrylic painting genre, 32

"copyright," customary law and, 100,
    128–129

Costello, Peter, 77

"country" and landscape, 14, 130, 135,
    140; Aboriginal conception of, 9, 11;
    abstraction and, 101–102; acrylic paints
    and, 32; color and, 25; cultural
    devastation and, 133–134; Dreaming
    and, 12; gender and, 75–76; images
    and, 70–71; Kathleen Petyarre and, 11,
    12–13; sacredness and, 52; wilderness,
    141

courts, justice and, 115–116

crafts, indigenous, 28

crime and punishment: child abuse, 49,
    76–77, 87–88, 92–94; customary law
    and, 119; domestic violence, 94; sexual
    violence and, 77, 87–88, 92–94, 127

Crow Nation, 131–132, 134, 136

cubism, 22

cultural authenticity: market forces and,
    46–47; origins of acrylic painting
    genre, 32–33, 40; postcolonial
    experience and, 62; Western aesthetics
    and, 4–5

cultural context: Aboriginal art and, 41;
    fine art markets and, 39–40, 45–52;
    images and, 64–68; museums and,
    52–56; photojournalism and, 68–73;
    translation and cultural exchange,
    58–60, 62; Western aesthetics and,
    62, 64

cultural devastation, 33, 35, 131–134

cultural differences: color theory, 21, 26;
    common law and, 107; conceptualizing
    time and space, 9, 11; research
    products and, 124–129

cultural exchange: Aboriginal art and,
    16; Abstract Expressionism and, 18; art
    and, 3; batik designs and, 28, 30; color
    and, 20, 27; cultural knowledge and,
    42–43; images and, 45; origins of
    acrylic painting genre, 30, 35;
    translation and, 58–60, 62

cultural knowledge: anthropology and,
    42–43; artistic judgments and, 38–39;
    collecting and, 56; common law and,
    106–107; "copyright" and, 100;
    customary law and, 128–129; discovery
    process and, 123–124

cultural narratives, 40

164   *Index*

curatorial issues, museums and, 54, 56

customary law: Aboriginal art and, 41; assimilationist policies and, 49; common law and, 106, 109, 119; "copyright," 100; "country" and landscape, 105; cultural devastation and, 131–132; land claims and, 104; male privilege and, 119; racism and, 121; sexual violence and child abuse, 93

dance, 12, 75

death, Abstract Expressionism and, 138

"death of art," 137–138

Deger, Jennifer, 43

De Kooning, Willem, 138

Deleuze, Gilles: abstraction and, 142; art as a commodity and, 146–147; "logic of sensation," 17, 18, 27; origins of acrylic painting genre, 31

democracy, justice and, 115

department stores, museums and, 54

Derrida, Jacques, 117–118

desert country spinifex, 14

desert grasses, 143

Desert painting. *See* Aboriginal art

desire, productions of representation, 66

Detmold, Michael, 107

difference, painting, 141–142

Diprose, Rosalyn, 11

Discovery Grants Scheme, 123–129

discovery process, law and, 123–129

discrimination, personal responsibility and, 91

disenchantment, 136–137

domestic violence, 94. *See also* child abuse; sexual violence

dotting techniques, 8

Dowling, Julie, 82

Dreaming: Aboriginal art and, 15; Aboriginal language and, 8–9; abstraction and, 17–18; career as artist and, 7–8; color and, 25; common law and, 106; "country" and landscape, 9, 11, 15–16; cultural devastation and, 132–133; Kathleen Petyarre and, 8, 12–13; modern Aboriginal aesthetic and, 13, 15

dreams, 11–12, 68

Duchamp, Marcel, 54

dysphoria, 81–82

earth tones, 26, 32–33

economic development, 37

economic exchanges, 13, 16, 99–102

economic value: Aboriginal art and, 40–41, 46; cultural context and, 45–47, 49

eco-tourism, 62

ego-ideal, the, 134, 136

empiricism, native title and, 109

Emu Dreaming, 132–134

Emu Dreaming and Bedford Downs Massacre (Bedford), 133–134

End of Art theory, 1, 18, 137

equivalence, legibility and, 65

ethics: aesthetics and, 2; cultural devastation and, 131; discovery process and, 125; photojournalism and, 71–73

ethnicity, of cultural scholars, 42

ethnography, 41–42, 52, 56, 145

Eurocentric perspectives. *See* Western art and culture

fabric arts, 27–28, 29

faces, turtle-shell masks and, 112

Fallon, Kathleen, 89–91

family dynamics, 126

Fauvism, 20

Feminine and the Sacred, The (Clément and Kristeva), 79

feminism and feminist theory: Aboriginal art and, 16, 96–97, 123–129; gender politics and, 77; Germaine Greer and, 87–89; law and, 123-129

"Feminist Theory Meets Indigenous Art," 96–97, 123

fine art markets: cultural context and, 39–40, 45–52; origins of acrylic painting genre, 31–32

form. *See* line and form

Foucault, Michel, 115–116

Francis Bacon: The Logic of Sensation (Deleuze), 142

Frankenthaler, Helen, 39

Freud, Sigmund, 12

Gage, John, 21, 23, 26

gender: Aboriginal culture and, 76–77, 79; Abstract Expressionism and, 138–139; color and, 22; "country" and landscape, 75–76; feminism and feminist theory, 16, 77, 87–89, 96–97, 123–129; law and, 121, 123; *Mabo v the State of Queensland (No. 2)* (1992) and, 119; race and racism, 84–91, 96–97; representation and, 91–94; sacredness of children and, 79–82, 84

generational differences, customary law and, 129

genocide, 82, 113, 133

global economy, 3, 4, 46–47

government funding, Aboriginal art and, 37

grants, discovery process and, 124–125, 126–127

Greenberg, Clement, 22

Greer, Germaine, 85–89

Griffiths, Peggy, 78

Hargraves, Lily Nungarrayi, 74

Hass, Marjorie, 113–114

Herbert, Myra Nungarrayi, 74

Hockney, David, 32

Hodges, Christopher, 141, 147

Hodgkin, Howard, 32

Hoheisal, Horst, 113–114

Holocaust, the, 113–114

Homage to a Square (Albers), 23

Honey Ant Dreaming mural, 30, 35

housing, 120

Howard, John, 84–85

Huggins, Jackie, 127

Icon for a Stolen Child (Dowling), 82

iconography: children and, 82, 84; images and, 70, 71; modern Aboriginal aesthetic and, 15; motherhood and, 80–81

Idagi, Ricardo, 110, 111–112, 114–115

identity, 81, 134

images: abstraction and, 146–147; children and, 81; cultural context and, 58, 64–68; cultural exchange and, 45; inherent value of, 40; nature and, 139, 141; photojournalism, 68–73

inherent value, art and, 39–40; Aboriginal art and, 46; abstraction and, 148–149; disenchantment and, 137–138; *Yuendumu Doors* and, 99–102

intellectual property, 100–102, 129

Interpretation of Dreams (Freud), 12
"Intervention, the," 85–91

Jirrawun Arts group, 132–133, 134
Johnson, Vivien, 7–8, 30
justice, 108, 115–116

Karrku red color, 21
Kean, John, 30
Klein, Melanie, 80
Klein, Yves, 21, 54
Kngwarreye, Emily Kame, 7; Aboriginal
    aesthetic and, 13, 15; abstraction and,
    139, 142; art as a commodity and,
    144–149; artistic judgments and, 38;
    batik designs and, 27–28; cultural
    knowledge and, 43; feminist theory
    and, 123; meaning and, 76; photographs
    and, 129
Koons, Jeff, 39
Kristeva, Julia, 65, 68, 79–82
kurruwarri, *Yuendumu Doors* and, 99–100

land claims, 35, 102–103; Aboriginal art
    and, 41; assimilationist policies and,
    49; law and, 99–102, 119, 128; origins
    of acrylic painting genre, 40; personal
    responsibility and, 92. *See also* native
    title
landscape. *See* "country" and landscape
landscape art, modern Aboriginal
    aesthetic and, 15
Langton, Marcia: apartheid and, 116–117;
    apologies from Australian government
    and, 85; art as a commodity and, 62;
    customary law and, 119; Germaine
    Greer and, 85–86, 88; personal
    responsibility and, 92–93

language: children and, 80, 81; Dreamtime
    and, 8–9; signification and, 81–82;
    translation and, 58–60, 62
law: Aboriginal art and, 99–105;
    apartheid and, 116–119, 121, 123; art as a
    commodity and, 144–149; common
    law, 106–109, 111–112; conflict of, 19;
    Discovery Grants Scheme and,
    123–129; memory and judgment,
    112–116; radical difference and, 131–134,
    136–139, 141–142, 144
Lear, Jonathan, 131–132, 134, 136–137
Lechte, John, 141–142
legibility, equivalence and, 65
Lévi-Strauss, Claude, 145
line and form, 21–22, 23, 142
"Little Children are Sacred" report, 49,
    76–77, 94
logic, of images, 64–66, 68
"logic of sensation," 17, 18, 27
loss, memory and, 113–114

Mabo, Eddie, 103
Mabo v the State of Queensland (No. 2) (1992),
    103, 104, 106–107, 119
Mackenzie, Queenie, 132
"Mackerel sky over Tanami Desert," xiv
Magaram le-op — (Idagi), 111–112
male privilege, 119
Mandela, Nelson, 118
maps, Aboriginal art and, 15
market forces: Aboriginal art and, 41,
    46–47; advertising images and, 65;
    Australian art community and, 50;
    "carpetbagging" and, 47, 49; color
    and, 20–21; museums and, 54; origins
    of acrylic painting genre, 33, 35, 37;
    tourist merchandise, 36; value of art

and, 3, 148. *See also* commodities, art
  as; fine art markets
marketing, museums and, 56
mass media, 20
Matisse, Henri, 23
meaning: Abstract Expressionism and,
  138–139; abstraction and, 149; logic of
  images and, 65; sacredness of children
  and, 82, 84; translation and, 58–60, 62;
  women artists and, 76
Memorial Stone Archive (Hoheisal), 113–114
memory and judgment, 112–116, 133
Mengil, Judy, 151
mental maps, 11
Merleau-Ponty, Maurice, 22, 25–26
metaphysics, racism and, 118
Michaels, Eric: artistic judgments and,
  38; color and, 21; "country" and
  landscape, 15, 105; cultural knowledge
  and, 43; Fred Myers and, 42; images
  and, 70–71; *Yuendumu Doors* and, 99–102
mise en discours, 39
modernism, 20, 21, 22, 136, 144–149
Moffatt, Tracey, 69
Morphy, Howard, 9, 13
motherhood, 79–81, 84
Mountain Devil Lizard (Petyarre), 8
mountain devil lizards, 10, 11
Musée du quai Branly, 39, 46, 58
Museum of Modern Art (New York),
  144–145
museums: Aboriginal art exhibitions and,
  40–41; cultural context and, 46, 52–56;
  market forces and, 47; primitive art
  and, 144–145
Myers, Fred, 27, 41–43
mystery, abstraction and, 149
mythology, art appreciation and, 39, 40

Namatjira, Albert, 32
Nampitjin, Eubena, 22
Napanangka, Makinti, 22
Napangardi, Dorothy, 75, 123
narrative, 41, 65
national identity, 56, 62
National Museum of Women in the
  Arts, 41
nation states, 116, 117
Native Americans, 131–132, 134, 136
native title: apartheid and, 118; common
  law and, 108, 119; land claims and,
  103–104; racism and, 121. *See also* land
  claims
natural law, 117
nature, images and, 139, 141
Neill, Rosemary, 87–88
nervous system, color and, 26
news media, 67, 68–73
Nicholls, Christine, 11
Ningamara, Phyllis, 151
"noble savage," racism and, 86
Noland, Kenneth, 23
nomadic peoples, land claims and, 104

objectivity, photojournalism and, 69, 70
oil paints, 32
"On Collecting Art and Culture"
  (Clifford), 56
On Rage (Greer), 85–89
ownership, of art, 38–39

Painting Culture (Myers), 27
Papunya: A Place Made After the Story
  (Bardon), 30, 33
Papunya artists, 30, 35, 37, 132
Papunya Painting (Kean), 30
Paydirt (Fallon), 89–91

personal responsibility, 86, 91, 93

personal taste, art appreciation and, 55

Petyarre, Gloria, 7

Petyarre, Kathleen, 7; Aboriginal aesthetic and, 13, 15; artistic judgments and, 38; Dreaming and, 8, 9; feminist theory and, 123; landscape and, 11

philosophy, Western, 134, 136–138, 146

"Photographic Message, The" (Barthes), 68–69

photographs, customary law and, 128, 129

photojournalism, 68–73

Piccinini, Patricia, 39

plagiarism, 38–39

Plenty Coups (Crow chief), 131, 134

plurality, global economy and, 4

polemics, 85–89

political correctness, 88–89

political dimensions: Aboriginal art and, 2; apologies from Australian government and, 85; feminism and, 87; gender politics and, 77; of modern art world, 16, 53; self-determination and personal responsibility, 92–93; turtle-shell masks and, 112

popular justice, reason and, 115–116

Possum & Wallaby Dreaming mural (Jagamara), 83

postcolonial experience: Aboriginal art and, 62, 64; Aboriginal culture and, 49–50, 76–77, 79; apartheid and, 116–119, 121, 123; color and, 25; Germaine Greer and, 85–89; textual metaphors and, 59

postmodernism, 18, 40, 144

power and truth, translation and, 60

pragmatism, common law and, 107–108

primitive art, 13, 16, 17, 26, 31, 144–145

privacy rights, 129

property rights, 129

psychology: abstraction and, 144; of color, 21, 25–26, 27; Dreaming and, 12; identity and, 134; images and, 68; motherhood and, 80

Pwerle, Minnie, 7

race and racism: apartheid and, 117–118; common law and, 108–109, 121; gender and, 84–91, 96–97; law and, 121, 123; *Paydirt* (Fallon) and, 89–91

Rachjman, John, 1, 18–19, 146–147

radical difference, law and, 131–134, 136–139, 141–142, 144

Radical Hope: Ethics in a Time of Cultural Devastation (Lear), 131–132

rage, Aboriginal men and, 85–89

reality: photographs and, 68–73, 129; productions of representation of, 66

"Real World": Aboriginal art and, 2, 64; color and, 26–27; justice and, 116; Kathleen Petyarre and, 12–13; Western aesthetics and, 3–5

reason: disenchantment and, 137; logic of images and, 66; popular justice and, 115–116

representation: art theory and, 1; gender and, 91–94; photojournalism and, 72; production of, 65–66; "Real World" and, 2

research, models of, 123–125

research products: as commodities, 125–126; cultural differences and, 124–129; financial accountability and, 125, 126

Rogers, Nanette, 93

Rothko, Mark, 17, 141–142, 145
Rudd, Kevin, 84
Ryan, Judith, 19–20, 111, 147

sacredness: Aboriginal art and, 5, 50, 52; Abstract Expressionism and, 138; art appreciation and, 66, 68; of children, 79–82, 84; cultural context and, 53–54; gender and, 79–80; museums and, 55; origins of acrylic painting genre, 35, 37; photojournalism and, 70
sales. *See* market forces; value of art
saltpans, 24
scarcity, market forces and, 50
Scarred for Life (Moffatt), 69
scholarship, ethnicity and, 42
science: of color, 23, 25–26; discovery process and, 124; images and, 68
self-determination, 77, 92, 93
semiotics, 59–60, 80
"sensation," 18, 19, 26, 27
separation, 81–82
September 11 terror attacks, 70, 71
sexism, racism and, 90–91
sexual violence, 77, 87–88, 92–94, 127
Shimmering Screens, 43
signification, 80, 81–82, 118
"sit down" money. *See* welfare payments
Smith, Terry, 18, 144–145
"social contract," 109
social responsibility, 37–38
souvenirs, museums and, 54
sovereignty, common law and, 107
spirituality, color and, 27
Stella, Frank, 23
Stengers, Isabelle, 124
stolen generations: Aboriginal culture and, 77, 79; apologies, from Australian government and, 84–85; child abuse and sexual violence, 76–77, 87–88; sacredness of children and, 82, 84
Sturmer, John von, 141
surrealism, 22
Sutton, Peter, 15, 86, 116
synaesthesia, 26

"Talking Back to the White Woman" (Huggins), 127
Tanami Desert, xiv
Tasman, Molly Napurrurla, 74
Tasman, Rosie Napurrurla, 74
technology, advertising images and, 64–65
terra nullius legal doctrine, 101, 102–103; apartheid and, 117, 118, 121; common law and, 108–109; "country" and landscape, 105; wilderness and, 141
textual metaphors, translation and, 58, 59–60
Thomas, Rover, 25, 132
time and space, conceptualizing, 9, 11, 21, 65
timelessness, of art, 53–54
Timms, Freddy, 25
"title deeds," 35
titles, law and, 149
Tjapaltjarri, Clifford Possum, 43
Torres Strait Islanders, 103, 111–112
tourism, 28, 57, 62, 114
tourist merchandise, 36, 61
Toyotas, value of art and, 100–101
traditional colors, Aboriginal art and, 25
transcendental meaning, 18
translation and cultural exchange, 58–60, 62, 64, 144
"Trapped in the Aboriginal Reality Show" (Langton), 86

trauma, memory and judgment, 113–115
treaties, land claims and, 103
trial by ordeal, 115
Turkey Creek Airfield, 51
Turkey Creek style, 133
Turkey Dreaming, 132–134
turtle-shell masks, 110, 111–112, 114–115

ultramarine, color of, 20–21
Uluru, 63, 122
Untitled (Kngwarreye), 141, 142
Utopia, Australia, 7–8

value of art, 39–40; Aboriginal art
    and, 46; abstraction and, 148–149;
    disenchantment and, 137–138;
    Yuendumu Doors and, 99–102
values, cultural context and, 47

wage employment, 49–50
wangarr (Dreaming), 8, 9
Warhol, Andy, 39, 54
Warlpiri artists, 2–3, 74, 99–102
watercolors, 32
Watson, Judy, 22
Watson, Tommy, 37–38
welfare payments, 76, 77, 79, 92

Western aesthetics: Aboriginal art and,
    13, 15; color and, 20–23, 26; cultural
    authenticity and, 4–5; cultural context
    and, 62, 64; customary law and, 109;
    museums and, 52–54; "Real World"
    and, 3–5; translation and, 60
Western art and culture: Aboriginal
    art and, 20; collaborative artworks
    and, 39; dreams and, 11–12;
    motherhood and, 80; natural law and,
    117; primitive art and, 17–18;
    sacredness
    of children and, 84; "social contract"
    and, 109
Western worldview, 49–50, 62, 64
white Australians: personal responsibility
    and, 92–94; racism and, 89–91; stolen
    generations and, 87–88
White Out (Neill), 88
wilderness, 141
women artists, 74; Aboriginal art and,
    16; color and, 22; "country" and
    landscape, 75–76; sexism and racism,
    96–97

Young, Diane, 21
Yuendumu Doors, 30, 43, 99–102

Lydia Goehr and Daniel Herwitz, eds., *The Don Giovanni Moment: Essays on the Legacy of an Opera*

Robert Hullot-Kentor, *Things Beyond Resemblance: Collected Essays on Theodor W. Adorno*

Gianni Vattimo, *Art's Claim to Truth*, edited by Santiago Zabala, translated by Luca D'Isanto

John T. Hamilton, *Music, Madness, and the Unworking of Language*

Stefan Jonsson, *A Brief History of the Masses: Three Revolutions*

Richard Eldridge, *Life, Literature, and Modernity*

Janet Wolff, *The Aesthetics of Uncertainty*

Lydia Goehr, *Elective Affinities: Musical Essays on the History of Aesthetic Theory*

Christoph Menke, *Tragic Play: Irony and Theater from Sophocles to Beckett*, translated by James Phillips

György Lukács, *Soul and Form*, translated by Anna Bostock and edited by John T. Sanders and Katie Terezakis with an introduction by Judith Butler

Joseph Margolis, *The Cultural Space of the Arts and the Infelicities of Reductionism*

Herbert Molderings, *Art as Experiment: Duchamp and the Aesthetics of Chance, Creativity, and Convention*

Whitney Davis, *Queer Beauty: Sexuality and Aesthetics from Winckelmann to Freud and Beyond*

Gail Day, *Dialectical Passions: Negation in Postwar Art Theory*

Gerhard Richter, *Afterness: Figures of Following in Modern Thought and Aesthetics*